TALK
TRIGGERS

The Complete Guide to Creating
Customers with Word of Mouth

TALK TRIGGERS

The Complete Guide to Creating Customers with Word of Mouth

JAY BAER AND DANIEL LEMIN

Portfolio / Penguin

Portfolio / Penguin
An imprint of Penguin Random House LLC
375 Hudson Street
New York, New York 10014

Most Portfolio books are available at a discount when purchased in quantity for sales
promotions or corporate use. Special editions, which include personalized covers, excerpts,
and corporate imprints, can be created when purchased in large quantities. For more
information, please call (212) 572-2232 or email specialmarkets@penguinrandomhouse
.com. Your local bookstore can also assist with discounted bulk purchases using the
Penguin Random House corporate Business-to-Business program. For assistance in
locating a participating retailer, email B2B@penguinrandomhouse.com.

ISBN 9780525537274 (hardcover)
ISBN 9780525537281 (ebook)

33614080768129

Printed in the United States of America
10 9 8 7 6 5 4 3 2 1

BOOK DESIGN BY LUCIA BERNARD

CONTENTS

Foreword by Ted Wright   ix

SECTION 1   Why Word of Mouth Works   1

CHAPTER 1
Talk Is Cheap   3

CHAPTER 2
Steer the Conversation   13

CHAPTER 3
Same Is Lame   23

SECTION 2   The Four Talk Triggers Criteria   33

CHAPTER 4
Be Remarkable   41

CHAPTER 5
Be Relevant   51

CHAPTER 6
Be Reasonable   61

CHAPTER 7
Be Repeatable   71

SECTION 3 **The Five Types of Talk Triggers**   81

CHAPTER 8
Talkable Empathy   87

CHAPTER 9
Talkable Usefulness   95

CHAPTER 10
Talkable Generosity   105

CHAPTER 11
Talkable Speed   115

CHAPTER 12
Talkable Attitude   123

SECTION 4 **Create Talk Triggers in Six Steps**

CHAPTER 13
Gather Internal Insights   139

CHAPTER 14
Get Close to Your Customers   151

CHAPTER 15
Create Candidate Talk Triggers   163

CHAPTER 16
Test and Measure Your Talk Triggers   177

CHAPTER 17

Expand and Turn On   189

CHAPTER 18

Amplify Your Talk Trigger   201

CHAPTER 19

Create Your Next Talk Trigger   211

Appendix: Quick Reference Guide   221

Acknowledgments   233

Authors' Note   237

Notes   239

Index   253

FOREWORD BY TED WRIGHT

Two years ago, Jay gave us a new way to think about engaging adversaries online. And he did it with a phrase so simple and pithy I'm annoyed I didn't think of it myself. Even if you haven't read the book (and if you haven't, please get on that), just a small portion of its title tells you everything you need to know: *Hug Your Haters*. Any questions? And if you do need examples and processes that explain how to implement his wisdom, Jay's got it. Jay has the ability to convey complex concepts clearly while offering really practical action steps. We're all better off for it.

This is why I was so excited when Jay and Daniel Lemin said they were writing a book on a critical aspect of word-of-mouth marketing—the story shared between consumers. It is the book you are holding now. And it could not have come at a better time.

Back when Fizz pioneered the first word-of-mouth marketing firm in 2001, I was part of a team that was reintroducing America's stodgiest beer as the signature brand of urban hipsters. Only the nerdiest among us would mix words like "influencer" into everyday conversation. Now, every YouTuber with five hundred subscribers and an Instagram feed full of interesting lattes is an "influencer."

Now that it's become the most overused—and, I would argue, least understood—term in marketing, I often feel the need to correct people. That's when a plaid-suited angel pops up on my shoulder like some Great Gazoo (look it up), and I hear "hug your haters," or another of Jay's bons mots. That's when I take a breath and start again from a place of love. Or at least of mutual understanding.

As the pillars of paid advertising—both traditional and digital—continue to crumble, the marketing establishment is frantically trying to exploit the power of peer-to-peer recommendation, which we've long known to be the dominant force in driving purchase decisions. But recommendations only work when they're authentic. Rather than do the hard work of identifying actual influencers, many companies are taking the easy route: paying insane amounts of money to disposable social media stars with tons of authenticity but little real-life influence.

That's a bit like buying a bicycle when what you need is a motorcycle. Yes, they both have two wheels, a seat, and handlebars. But the moment you take a bicycle out on the highway, you know you've made a terrible mistake. The key to influencer marketing: Don't buy the bicycle.

The core of the problem is that most marketers are simply more comfortable dealing with media buyers than they are talking to consumers (you know, people). Decades of disintermediation have left them ill-prepared for the untidiness of word-of-mouth marketing, which is—at base—the art of talking to people. Buying a prime-time commercial slot is expensive but easy; sparking a conversation about your brand among a network of loosely connected humans is cheaper but infinitely more complex. It requires patience, faith, and agility, not traits that have traditionally been valued in CMOs.

It's easy to see the lure of social media celebrities to marketers who were raised in this environment. For a couple of bucks, anyone from a Kardashian to a Kewtie Pie will gladly toss up a #sponsored post featuring your product. But any decent word-of-mouth marketer will tell you: Real influencers rarely need to be paid. In fact, most of them can't be bought. It's a failure of our profession that so many marketers still don't get that.

Which brings me back to Jay and Daniel. What we need is someone who can break down the true word-of-mouth process into its basic components and explain it in terms that everyone can grasp. How do you start a conversation about your brand? How do you get closer to your customers? What is the difference between a fan and an advocate, and how do you convert one into the other? And why is an obsession with "going viral" probably not helpful for your brand? *Talk Triggers* covers all of that in swift, accessible language.

The power of what we do has become undeniable. Pabst Blue Ribbon, the stodgy beer brand I was referring to earlier, has long been a case study in reinvention. But the success of brands like Slack, CrossFit, Chipotle, Dropbox, Tesla, and Google have proved that word-of-mouth marketing creates not just customers but loyal, passionate advocates. Not surprisingly, marketers want to know more. And they are done being duped by the influencer industrial complex.

They are fortunate to have this book. In the pages ahead, Jay and Daniel will walk you through the first and most vital element of word-of-mouth marketing, the story friends will tell each other about your brand. Godin called it the "Purple Cow. " I called it the "talkable" part of your brand. Jay, flexing his talent for pithy phrasing, has dubbed it the "Talk Trigger. " It could be an unusually large menu, a cookie left on your hotel pillow, a hotline that connects customers directly to the CEO, or funny hold music. Whatever it is—and it can be almost anything—you need it to create word of mouth.

Yes, I wrote a book on word-of-mouth marketing, and yes, it sells very well, but now is a dangerous time for word-of-mouth marketing. On the one hand, our concepts and terminology have never been more mainstream. On the other hand, there have never been so many of the underwhelming laying claim to our craft. This book will help ensure that, when all is said and done, those with true understanding will be the ones left standing.

Tell your friends about it.

TALK TRIGGERS

The Complete Guide to Creating
Customers with Word of Mouth

SECTION 1

Why Word of Mouth Works

CHAPTER 1

Talk Is Cheap

Do you like chicken? Do you *really, really, really* like chicken? Do you like chicken as much as Jimmy Buffett likes the beach? If so, The Cheesecake Factory is your perfect restaurant.

Each of the chain's 200 locations offers 85 different chicken dishes. Unsurprisingly, given how many chicken dishes alone it includes, the menu itself runs 5,940 words long. That is more than 11 percent of the book you are about to read.

You might think that's too long, but for The Cheesecake Factory, it's just right. Why? Because the vastness of the restaurant's menu is so unusual that it compels conversation among its patrons. Menu breadth is its secret customer-acquisition weapon—it hides in plain sight, in the hands of each and every diner.

The menu at The Cheesecake Factory is a talk trigger: a built-in differentiator that creates customer conversations.

Every day consumers comment on the remarkable menu variety with a combination of bewilderment, awe, and frustration. Twitter alone produced this cross section of commentaries (and dozens more) about The Cheesecake Factory menu in early November 2017, riding along the digital winds like a smartphone-enabled messenger pigeon, spreading the word about the brand's core differentiator to many thousands of potential new customers:

Christopher
@potterhead0499

Follow ⌄

I've been to Cheesecake Factory a hundred times and I still haven't made it through the menu. #CheesecakeFactory

4:56 AM - 19 Nov 2017

Austin
@TheRisky_Ginger

Follow ⌄

The Cheesecake Factory menu is like a very weird book. It's the Ulysses of menus. People say they've read it, but no one's really finished it.

2:25 PM - 17 Nov 2017

Greg Mania ✓
@gregmania

Follow ⌄

what book do you want to see made into a movie? i want to see the Cheesecake Factory menu

7:26 PM - 17 Nov 2017

Like extravagant sunglasses at an Elton John concert, the menu is such an iconic part of The Cheesecake Factory experience that some customers refer to it that way:

> **CECE ✦**
> @cece24_lovesu
>
> (Follow) ∨
>
> My mom just said "we should go to the
> gigantic menu" and my dad was like "I hope
> you mean Cheesecake Factory" 💀
>
> 4:12 PM - 5 Nov 2017

The menu's benefit to The Cheesecake Factory's business is massive. Financial filings for the public company show that it spends just 0.20 percent of its total sales on advertising.

Darden Restaurants, a major competitor, operates Olive Garden, the Capital Grille, Yard House, and several other dining brands. Darden is roughly three times larger but spends 1,799 percent more on advertising (as a percentage of sales). In real dollars, Darden spends $268 million per year more in advertising than does The Cheesecake Factory.

The Cheesecake Factory doesn't have to buy awareness because its menu is remarkable enough to compel patrons to tell their friends, which in turn creates new customers. When you commit to a talk trigger like The Cheesecake Factory menu, that difference creates conversation that clones your customers, bringing you new revenue for free.

Researchers David Godes and Dina Mayzlin found that a single word-of-mouth conversation by a new customer leads to an almost $200 increase in restaurant sales. When that occurs repeatedly, you end up with The Cheesecake Factory, a multibillion-dollar company that barely pays to promote itself despite operating in a category that typically requires heavy advertising.

The Right Kind of Talk

You might be wondering: How often do customers really notice talk triggers? And more important: How much do those differentiators actually get discussed? After all, an operational strength that doesn't encourage conversation may grow repeat business from the original customer, but it does not create new customers at little to no cost. This pass-along effect—when customers tell your story almost involuntarily, turning themselves into volunteer marketers—is what makes word of mouth so delightfully impactful for companies that possess a talk trigger.

To better understand the impact of The Cheesecake Factory's talk triggers, we partnered with Audience Audit, a respected provider of consumer panel research, to identify hundreds of adults who had dined at a Cheesecake Factory location within the prior thirty days.

Respondents were asked, "Have you ever recommended The Cheesecake Factory to someone who was not specifically asking for recommendations, just because you were particularly pleased with your experience?" Among them, 66 percent had.

Perhaps even more impressive is our research finding that more than nine in ten customers discuss The Cheesecake Factory when directly asked for restaurant recommendations. Respondents were asked, "Have you ever suggested The Cheesecake Factory to someone who was specifically asking for a restaurant recommendation?" Nearly every patron of The Cheesecake Factory becomes an advocate when the opportunity arises.

It was immediately clear that diners at The Cheesecake Factory talk about the experience. But when these customers converse, do they discuss generalities (e.g., "The Cheesecake Factory has good food"), or do they discuss specifics?

The difference is important. Word-of-mouth impact is usually higher when the information exchanged is specific.

A consulting client of ours asked us an interesting question that you might also be wondering. She said, "What's the difference between a talk trigger and a unique selling proposition (USP)?" A USP is well-worn marketing shorthand defined as "a factor that differentiates a product from its competitors, such as the lowest cost, the highest quality, or the first-ever product of its kind."

Here's how we answered the client: "A USP is a feature, articulated with a bullet point, that is discussed in a conference room. A talk trigger is a benefit, articulated with a story, that is discussed at a cocktail party." A USP is important, but the problem is that almost every one of them has plenty of SP, and very little U. Sure, "quality food" and "good service" are selling propositions. But they aren't unique, and that atrophies word of mouth.

In our survey of The Cheesecake Factory customers, we asked this question two ways. First, we asked, "What do you typically mention about The Cheesecake Factory when you recommend it to someone?"

Sixty percent of customers said "food quality," which we classify

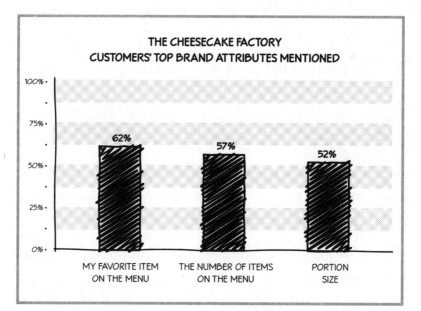

THE CHEESECAKE FACTORY
CUSTOMERS' TOP BRAND ATTRIBUTES MENTIONED

as general information—it's a USP. It's also not a particularly compelling or memorable story, because food quality is not in and of
itself a differentiator in the category. Many restaurants offer food
quality, so it doesn't have a tremendous amount of story power.

But the second-most mentioned aspect of the brand is the breadth
of the menu. Nearly four in ten customers said they've talked about
this differentiator. It's a talk trigger!

Second, we gave customers a list of attributes and then asked
them what they said about the restaurant. In this aided, prompted
scenario, the impact of menu breadth is even more pronounced.

When presented with this list, more than half of all surveyed customers said they have mentioned the number of menu items to someone else, the second-most common attribute discussed.

Customers of The Cheesecake Factory notice the size of the menu
and discuss the size of the menu, propelling awareness and encouraging new patrons to visit the restaurant for the first time. The company has successfully turned its customers into volunteer marketers.
And you can do the same.

You Can't Afford to Ignore Word of Mouth

Word of mouth is perhaps the most effective and cost-effective way
to grow any company. Yet we often take it for granted, like free coffee refills or another U2 album.

One of the reasons we wrote this book is to solve this mystery: As
consumers, we all know how impactful word-of-mouth recommendations are, and we have firsthand experiences with them consistently. But in our jobs, we give very little thought to making sure our
products activate word-of-mouth recommendations. Why and how
is this the case?

Perhaps businesspeople don't actually believe in the power of word of mouth? That hardly seems possible given the available evidence.

A very detailed examination of the impact of word of mouth by Engagement Labs in 2017 found that 19 percent of all consumer purchases in the United States were directly caused by offline or online word-of-mouth activity. That's approximately $10 trillion of economic impact. And a lot more than 19 percent of purchases are influenced by word of mouth, even if consumers don't fully realize or recognize it (the same way that people unwittingly hum Katy Perry songs in the shower).

Word of mouth isn't applicable only to consumer spending either. In fact, a study conducted by Blanc & Otus and G2Crowd discovered that the impact of recommendations and referrals in business-to-business (B2B) scenarios is actually far greater, due to the considered nature of most purchases, the high average prices, and the limited number of total customers.

And right now, word of mouth is more effective and important than ever for these three reasons:

1. It is **hyper-relevant**. The recommender customizes the recommendation to fit the receiver's perceived needs. No other form of marketing is as personalized, and consumers increasingly desire personalization.
2. Positive word of mouth **saves the recipient time** by giving him or her a referral and recommendation, eliminating some or all of the research needed to make a sound decision.
3. When offered by consumers to one another, word of mouth is **independent**, as the talker has no financial interest in the sale of the service. A consumer's independence adds credibility and persuasiveness to the recommendation. This trust advantage is the key to why word of mouth is so crucial today. Fundamentally, we trust businesses and organizations less than ever, and we trust people more than ever.

According to the research firm Nielsen, 83 percent of Americans trust recommendations from friends and family, and 60 percent trust online reviews—an important form of asynchronous word of mouth. In comparison, just 52 percent of citizens trust businesses globally, according to Edelman Public Relations, and in sixteen of the twenty-eight countries surveyed, less than half the respondents say they trust companies.

Regardless of the size, shape, category, and the history of your business, the reality is that half your customers do not believe you. Author and keynote speaker David Horsager says trust is "a company's most important asset." He's right, but the best distribution vehicle for that trust is not the company itself but rather its customers. We're in an era where trust matters more than truth, and the truth is that your customers simply don't trust you as much as they trust each other.

People have the power now in ways that would have been unthinkable just a few years ago. This is why the time for talk triggers has never been better—or more necessary. Businesses' ability to unilaterally dictate consumer attitudes and subsequent purchases and loyalties is fraying like the hem of a cheap dress.

The best organizations are running ahead of this shift, purposefully crafting differentiators that get customers to tell authentic, visceral, trusted stories about the business and its products or services—stories that create new customers through referrals and recommendations.

In his book *The Referral Engine*, John Jantsch, founder of Duct Tape Marketing, researched twelve hundred small and medium-size businesses and discovered that 63 percent of business owners believed that more than half their overall revenue came from referrals. Yet 80 percent of those respondents had no defined system for generating those referrals. Jantsch told us in an interview, "Today, most referrals happen by accident."

Jantsch figures that 1 percent or less of all businesses have a written plan for creating chatter. One hundred percent of businesses care about word of mouth, but less than 1 percent have a plan for achieving it. That's why we wrote *Talk Triggers*.

There are many terrific books about word of mouth and its value. Commentary from the authors of many of them is included here, and we cite their research and conclusions throughout. But what we set out to do with *Talk Triggers* is to provide more structure and scaffolding to give you a clear, linear, understandable, and achievable system for harnessing the extraordinary power of word of mouth. We've tried to create a book that doesn't just tell you why talk triggers are so vital but also explains how to actually make them work, beginning the day you finish reading.

Based on our research and the findings of dozens of other authors and academics, mixed with our forty-five years of combined experience as marketing consultants to hundreds of organizations and dozens of *Fortune* 500 brands, we have developed the talk triggers framework for how to create word of mouth in any business.

We unveil this framework here, in four sections.

This first section discusses the importance and economic impact of word of mouth and examines why the overwhelming majority of organizations take a laissez-faire approach to it.

The second section demonstrates each of the four criteria that need to be present for an operational differentiator to function as a consistent conversation catalyst.

The third section unveils the five different types of talk triggers that can be developed and optimized to turn customers into volunteer marketers.

The final section includes a comprehensive six-step process for identifying, analyzing, testing, measuring, and operationalizing talk triggers in any organization.

We've also included a quick reference guide in the appendix that summarizes key research, themes, and lessons. This handy reference guide was very popular with readers of our best-selling books *Youtility*, *Hug Your Haters*, and *Manipurated*. We hope you like it,

too, and find it to be a time-saver when you want to refer back to
Talk Triggers after your first reading.

Additional resources, including videos, handouts, presentation
templates, worksheets, and more, will also help you to create talk
triggers and put them into practice. So before we continue, please
invest ten seconds and go to TalkTriggers.com to access the bonus
materials we've created that will help you along the way. You might
even discover one of *our* talk triggers while you're there.

CHAPTER 2

Steer the Conversation

We hope you agree that word of mouth is critical and can be a most powerful catapult for business growth. Yet it remains vastly underdiscussed and underutilized. Is word-of-mouth marketing the kale of business? We all know it's good for us, yet most of us eschew or ignore it anyway.

Maybe the reason for the huge discrepancy between word-of-mouth importance and word-of-mouth strategy is that it is, by definition, harder to see and understand than most other advertising and marketing avenues? It's like affinity for Miley Cyrus; you know it's out there, but you can't quite put a finger on it.

When we asked this question of Jonah Berger, professor and author of *Contagious*, he agreed that the ephemeral nature of word of mouth presents some cause-and-effect challenges for many marketers and business owners: "People know how to buy paid media. They say, 'Here is my money, I will exchange it for this many impressions of paid media.' It's a challenge for people to think about how to buy word of mouth, because you can't necessarily buy it. You can shape it, you can encourage it, you can drive it, but you can't buy it. So I think that lack of control has made some companies and organizations feel like it's more challenging to acquire."

There is also a belief in some corners of the business world that social media *is* word of mouth, or that social media has replaced word of mouth as the driver of consumer awareness and preference. It isn't. And it hasn't. Social media is a critical component of the overall word-of-mouth equation. In fact, offline and online conversations are almost exactly equal in size, according to new research from Engagement Labs. Today, online and offline word of mouth each drive almost precisely the same economic impact; they just tend to do so in different circumstances.

"I think it is vitally important for brand marketers to understand that the rise of social media is real, it's undeniable, and it's an important channel. But interestingly, it has not knocked the value of [offline] word of mouth off the table," says Ed Keller, coauthor of *The Face-to-Face Book* and CEO of Engagement Labs.

Keller says people's motivations to talk about brands on social media are different than their rationale for offline word of mouth. "Social media is heavily driven by people's desire for social signaling. It says something about me when I post something on social media," he asserts.

We're sure you witness this in your own orbit. Your friends post short videos of the amazing concert they went to last night but conveniently forget to post anything when they attend the washed up 1970s rock band reunion show at the local bowling alley and casino. On social media, everyone's life is curated, like a museum of the mundane. Offline, we still feel capable of showing our real selves and our real feelings about brands and experiences.

It may seem like the narrower reach of face-to-face conversations would limit the net impact of word of mouth, but in reality, the persuasiveness of these exchanges more than overcomes their private nature. Most researchers conclude that offline word of mouth is more persuasive than an online variant. Fifty-eight percent of consumers ascribe high credibility to the information they hear from others during a spoken conversation, and 50 percent say they are very likely to buy as a result of that conversation, according to research from the Keller Fay Group.

There are some circumstances, however, when online social media is actually the most impactful form of word of mouth. When booking a vacation, for example.

Not to mention that successful and memorable word-of-mouth recommendations are passed along like a baton in a relay race. Says Ted Wright, author of *Fizz*, "Word of mouth spreads from an influencer's mouth at a rate of eight factorial annually: 40,370 people each year." A single diner, entranced by a gigantic menu, can impact the brand perception of 40,369 other potential customers.

The consultancy McKinsey deduced in its own research, "Typically, messages passed within tight, trusted networks have less reach but greater impact than those circulated through dispersed communities—in part, because there's usually a high correlation between people whose opinions we trust and the members of networks we most value. That's why old-fashioned kitchen table recommendations and their online equivalents remain so important. After all, a person with 300 friends on Facebook may happily ignore the advice of 290 of them. It's the small, close-knit network of trusted friends that has the real influence."

Even though word of mouth in social media represents just half the overall impact of customer conversations, companies spend billions of dollars each year on social media programs, and nearly every company has at least an outline of a social media strategy.

In the United States alone, direct spending on social media

advertising increased from $4.3 billion in 2012 to an anticipated $23.6 billion in 2019. This increase does not account for the many billions of dollars in labor costs to staff social media roles in companies nor the billions of dollars in software licenses and other operational expenditures necessary to execute social media tactics on a day-to-day basis.

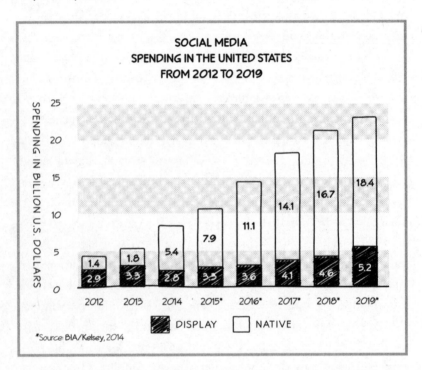

SOCIAL MEDIA
SPENDING IN THE UNITED STATES
FROM 2012 TO 2019

SPENDING IN BILLION U.S. DOLLARS

Year	Display	Native
2012	2.9	1.4
2013	3.3	1.8
2014	2.8	5.4
2015*	3.5	7.9
2016*	3.6	11.1
2017*	4.1	14.1
2018*	4.6	16.7
2019*	5.2	18.4

DISPLAY   NATIVE

*Source: BIA/Kelsey, 2014

Andy Sernovitz, cofounder of the Word of Mouth Marketing Association (WOMMA) and author of the pioneering book *Word of Mouth Marketing*, warns us not to substitute social media noise for real word of mouth.

"Social media is great for speed, but it's just a tool. Word of mouth is hard. Earning respect, earning recommendations, or launching deep ideas require a genuinely good company to provide a talkworthy experience," Sernovitz told us.

Why are social media conversations only one part of the

word-of-mouth package? They are very much the most identifiable and visible elements of customer conversation. The public nature of social media chatter means that word of mouth in those venues is findable in an instant, unlike offline word of mouth, which requires specific research such as we conducted for The Cheesecake Factory and other brands.

Because online conversations are public, we have used them throughout *Talk Triggers* to demonstrate the success that word of mouth is generating for the businesses and organizations profiled in this book.

DoubleTree by Hilton is one such example. It has been creating conversations for decades, both online and offline, based on a simple yet extraordinarily effective differentiator.

DoubleTree by Hilton

Any restaurant in the world could conceivably mimic The Cheesecake Factory and offer a menu that is 5,940 words long, provided it could tackle the extreme supply chain, logistics, and training challenges presented by that differentiator. Practically no business does, however.

The same is true for the hospitality category. There are dozens—perhaps hundreds—of hotel chains in the world. Yet very few have a talk trigger.

DoubleTree by Hilton is an exception, and the brand's talk trigger began in 1986. Can you guess what it is?

We'll wait.
Go ahead.
It's OK.

That's right, DoubleTree's talk trigger is a chocolate chip cookie.

For more than thirty years, the hotelier has been providing warm chocolate chip cookies to guests. Initially conceived as a turndown service, team members would hand-deliver a warm cookie each evening.

In 1995 the service was modified so that the cookie is presented when the guest checks in to the property and has continued unabated ever since. Today, across the brand's more than 500 global locations, they give away an astonishing 75,000 cookies every day. In the United States, the Christie Cookie Company in Nashville, Tennessee, is the exclusive provider of the dough and recipe and has been since 1996. Since then, DoubleTree hotels have given away 384 million cookies. They are baked every day, in each hotel.

Consistency of the cookie experience is massively important to the brand. The recipe is precisely the same worldwide, and the cookies are baked uniformly throughout the United States. If you have a craving but aren't keen on a hotel stay, Americans can buy cookies and have them shipped via www.doubletreecookies.com. The brand even sells the dough to bake them yourself, if you prefer.

In addition to the cookies offered at check-in, the hotels often celebrate and utilize cookies in other ways, emphasizing the talk trigger. Many of the chefs in DoubleTree restaurants create dishes with the cookies, for instance.

The cookies matter a lot to DoubleTree, as Stuart Foster, VP of global brands for Hilton, made clear. "We see the cookie really as a symbol of hospitality and a very strong symbol, which a lot of brands don't have." Foster told us that "DoubleTree is known for its warm welcome. We are the welcoming brand. The cookie is the first symbol in a series of welcoming moments that you're going to get. DoubleTree is all about our care culture and service experience, and our team members have a lot of pride in what they do and we think that's how DoubleTree is differentiated in its category, but we're also very lucky to have this cookie [which is a] symbol that resonates with people almost immediately. It has this cult following."

He notes that the cult following isn't just among customers. "It's not just the guests who love it. Team members really rally behind the cookie as well, just as much and sometimes more."

They are clearly a passion point inside and outside the brand, but how well do all these cookies actually function as a talk trigger and creator of word of mouth? Very.

We partnered again with Audience Audit to survey guests who have stayed at a DoubleTree hotel in the past ninety days, asking the same questions that we asked about The Cheesecake Factory.

Remarkably, almost seven in ten customers have recommended DoubleTree hotels just because they were pleased with the experience.

Nearly 90 percent of guests staying at a DoubleTree hotel in the past three months say they've mentioned the brand when asked about a hotel.

DoubleTree customers also commonly discuss the talk trigger of a warm chocolate chip cookie provided for free at check-in. More than one-third of customers say they have mentioned the cookie to someone else. This makes the cookie differentiator the third most mentioned feature behind "service" and "cleanliness."

Similar to The Cheesecake Factory's customers mentioning "food quality" most often, references to "service" and "cleanliness" are certainly indicators of a quality experience but have middling story weight unless accompanied by a truly exceptional scenario. Many hotels are clean. It's a USP, not a talk trigger.

When provided a list of hotel attributes to consider, nearly 70 percent of DoubleTree guests mentioned they had talked about the chocolate chip cookie, ranking just behind friendliness of staff (a similar feature of the hospitality approach that spawned the cookie) and comfortable beds.

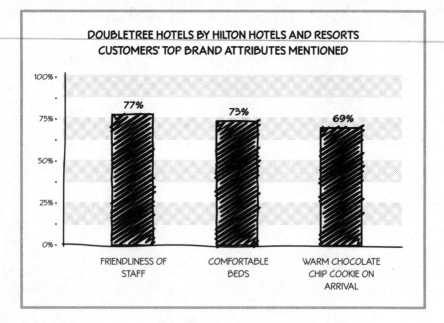

The talkability of hotel beds is well known. In fact, while we would argue that DoubleTree is the only large hotel chain to possess a meaningful talk trigger today (boutique hotelier Graduate Hotels has an excellent one we'll show you later), others have attempted to create one and either failed to generate sufficient chatter, or were unable to protect the idea.

Westin Hotels, for instance, for several years emphasized its Heavenly Bed and promised a talkably better sleep experience. Alas, multiple other chains made massive investments in sleep technology, and the trigger became indefensible. Once it's not a differentiator, the talk trigger loses its edge and becomes a general advantage like "food quality" and "service." Not unimportant but also not strong enough to be remembered and passed along either.

DoubleTree sees this difference between general and specific attributes as well. Although the cookies are only the third most cited feature, they absolutely incite the deepest passion. "On our social media channels, any post that has the cookie tends to outperform everything else. People just love it," says Foster.

This simple reminder on Twitter, for instance, racked up more than six thousand likes and nearly seven hundred retweets:

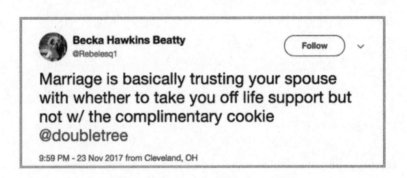

Guest Becka Hawkins Beatty put a fine point on the importance of the cookie with this tweet:

Becka Hawkins Beatty
@Rebelesq1

Follow ⌄

Marriage is basically trusting your spouse with whether to take you off life support but not w/ the complimentary cookie @doubletree

9:59 PM - 23 Nov 2017 from Cleveland, OH

These expressions of support add up, both online and offline, and it drives new customers as a result. Done well, talk triggers clone your customers. In every presentation we do about talk triggers, we show a picture of a chocolate chip cookie and ask the audience to shout out which company uses it as a differentiator. Knowledge of the cookie is pervasive!

And when we asked participants in our DoubleTree research to tell us what they remember about the brand, there were dozens of responses like this:

"First, oh my gosh, they give you warm, yummy cookies. And every time I stay there, they are always very nice."

Companies that deploy a talk trigger have a competitive advantage. And in this age when consumer chatter is manifestly trusted and influential, the real question is, Can you afford to NOT be purposeful and strategic any longer?

Our aim is to help you get intentional about your word of mouth—turning it from a program that runs on hope to a strategy powered by talk triggers. We want you to move from random word of mouth to robust word-of-mouth marketing.

We've already shown you examples of how differentiators can propel conversation. Yet the de facto approach to competition embraced by most businesses is to play "follow the leader" and copy what's working for others, instead of doing something memorably different. Mimicry is low risk but also low reward. Let's look at why "same is lame."

CHAPTER 3

Same Is Lame

A s we've seen from our research of the customers of brands such as The Cheesecake Factory and DoubleTree hotels, conversations will occur about core attributes like food quality and room cleanliness. For a differentiator to *keep spreading* beyond the first telling, however, it has to be inherently more interesting. It should be unexpected. It should be worthy of a story, meaning that it has to be intriguing enough to the recipient to be worth the exchange of time for information. We don't know you. But we do know what you've never done. You, Mr. or Ms. Reader, have never said to a friend or perfect stranger: "Let me tell you about a perfectly adequate experience I had recently!"

The best story—the most compelling and dynamic talk trigger— can set your business apart in ways that incremental upgrades to customer service or price reductions cannot.

It's often been said that advertising is a tax paid by unremarkable businesses. Talk triggers enable you to avoid that tax almost entirely, as The Cheesecake Factory, DoubleTree by Hilton, and many other case studies in this book demonstrate. But when businesses look solely at the very top players in their industries, they often see that tax being paid and assume it's the path to success. We disagree, especially if you are in any way a challenger brand that seeks to steal market share from a category leader—trying to do so without a talk trigger is like trying to pole-vault with a bowling ball tied to your ankle. It's doable in the strictest sense, but you're adding a degree of difficulty that is daunting and unnecessary.

The best way to create conversation is to have a selling proposition that is actually unique. After all, same is lame. We are physiologically conditioned to discuss what is different and to ignore average.

Author Seth Godin calls this the Purple Cow effect. And it's the key to creating a talk trigger that actually works, and it propels the story about your business from one customer to thousands of potential customers.

Why did a young David Bowie adopt the way-out-there Ziggy Stardust persona? Maybe he was just weird, but a more craven explanation is that he needed a talk trigger and knew that to spur conversation he'd need to defy established norms. In fact, an article in *Rolling Stone* magazine about the invention of Ziggy states that Bowie was "looking to out-glam and out-shock acts like Alice Cooper."

This probably makes intuitive sense to you, as a consumer. Yet we don't often emphasize the crafting of differences in business, and we may do so less than ever. Almost every company makes decisions that eliminate memorable differentiators, as you may have witnessed personally. Most businesses don't optimally benefit from word of mouth simply because they give patrons insufficient raw materials for conversation. In short, the story isn't good enough.

And lack of differentiation puts enormous pressure on your bottom line. When you fail to have a meaningful experiential differentiator, you are not only required to pay the tax on unremarkability in the form of increased advertising spending, but also you have a much harder time charging any sort of premium for whatever you offer.

If your product isn't talkable, then cost becomes the sole basis of comparison. "Customers will always find a point of distinction. Therefore, if you fail to outline one for them in compelling fashion, they will go to the worst possible distinguisher for you: price," wrote keynote speaker and differentiation consultant Scott McKain in his book *Create Distinction*. "Being different, standing out, getting noticed in a sea of sameness is vital to an organization's sustained growth and profitability," he added.

Today's business wisdom is often anchored by the edict to improve customer experience in every respect. That's wise and admirable on one hand, as poor customer experience and customer service diminishes loyalty and customer retention. Jay Baer authored an entire book, *Hug Your Haters*, about this scenario. On the other hand, a focus on improving customer experience makes it more difficult to create and propagate a truly differentiated talk trigger. This is because customer experience enhancements are about being better, not being different. And as author and motivational speaker Sally Hogshead says, when it comes to word of mouth, "different is better than better."

How much does the modern-day zeal to improve customer experience interfere with talk trigger development? A lot, given that 95 percent of leaders say providing a good customer experience is their top strategic priority. Three-quarters of them want to use customer experience as a competitive advantage.

And that's the problem. What they fail to understand is that improved customer experience is not a competitive advantage. If everyone has good food, what's your edge? If everyone has good service, is yours so much better that it's a deciding factor for potential customers? Nope.

We want to acknowledge here that people can and should be both satisfied and surprised. DoubleTree by Hilton does it every day. The product is great *and* everyone gets a cookie. It's not about having good customer experience or a talk trigger. You should have good customer experience first, so you stop losing frustrated customers like a leaky bucket, and then, once you have your operational house in order, go all-in on creating a talk trigger that stimulates conversation.

Talk triggers might seem, at this point, to be a nice-to-have—a fun augmentation to your operational and marketing approach that can drive some incremental customers your way. But in truth, talk triggers are far more important than that. In fact, the presence of a meaningful differentiator could mean the difference between the success and failure of the entire enterprise.

The Cheesecake Factory is about culinary adventure. Its talk trigger, a massive menu, amplifies this attribute. DoubleTree by Hilton is about warm welcomes. Its talk trigger, a cookie at check-in, amplifies this attribute.

Your talk trigger will work because your customers perceive it to be different from what they expect. But the best talk triggers work because they are distillates of the essence of your organization. In this sense, talk triggers are not marketing. They aren't a stunt or a campaign or a slogan. They are you. Of course, talk triggers create marketing advantages, but those marketing advantages aren't a consequence of empty sloganeering.

As Emanuel Rosen put it in *The Anatomy of Buzz Revisited*: "[T]he best buzz comes not from clever PR or advertising but rather from attributes inherent in the product or service itself."

The reality is that most of us who set out to craft a difference-maker fail to do so. We get sucked back into incremental advances and USPs that don't resonate. It is imperative to create a talk trigger that contains enough of the unexpected to cause conversation. Otherwise, what's the point?

We understand that it's hard. If it wasn't, why write (or read) this book? We'll talk more about being remarkable (in the definitional sense of being worthy of remark) in the next chapter.

But part of the problem is that "being different" is often thought to require no care or feeding. Most companies are content to let word of mouth just happen, expecting that randomly generated referrals will occur with sufficient volume and amplitude to sustain them. The businesses profiled in *Talk Triggers* take the exact opposite approach. They engage in word of mouth with intention. They have a plan and a purpose.

This is the difference between word of mouth and word-of-mouth marketing. As Ted Wright told us, "Word of mouth is just talking. Word-of-mouth marketing is the organizing of that talk and driving it in a particular way. It's doing something intentional."

In these pages we profile the best organizations—those whose talk triggers are the most effective, the ones where the customers literally say, "You will *not* believe what happened to me when . . ." Those organizations firmly believe that same is lame. For them, being different is part of the culture, and perhaps that's why they don't consider it a risk; it's just who and what they are.

That sounds exactly like WindsorONE.

WindsorONE Lumber

Says Sally Hogshead, "The brands in the least fascinating category have the opportunity to become the most fascinating because the bar is so much lower relative to them."

Family-owned specialty lumber company WindsorONE proves the accuracy of her statement every day. Based in Petaluma, California, WindsorONE may have the most strategic and effective word-of-mouth marketing program of any business we've studied. It's certainly the most comprehensive example of B2B word of mouth we've yet encountered.

Speaking of which, if you have ideas and examples of businesses with effective word-of-mouth marketing and talk triggers, please email us anytime at JayAndDaniel@TalkTriggers.com. We're always hungry for new stories!

Founded in 1972, Windsor Mill manufactures high-end trim boards for residential and commercial building applications. Its product line—WindsorONE—is made in the United States and targets serious wood craftspeople who are willing to pay a premium for quality.

The same way that The Cheesecake Factory has good food and DoubleTree by Hilton has comfortable beds, WindsorONE Lumber genuinely makes excellent wood trim. It's probably the best available. But being very good—even being the best—isn't inherently talkable. It's not a story; it's just an attribute—a bullet point on a brochure. It creates loyalty, but it doesn't compel conversation.

WindsorONE knew it needed more than quality to power word of mouth, especially in a challenging economic environment.

Director of Marketing Brian Bunt explains: "Basically, in 2007 and 2008, the housing market crashed and we weren't sure what we were going to do for marketing because we couldn't afford to do the more expensive ads and trade publications. And there was a lot of turmoil going on. We attended a class Andy Sernovitz held about word-of-mouth marketing, and we came up with some ideas."

One of its first initiatives was to encourage customers to call the company to receive a free T-shirt. Previously, for many years, WindsorONE had used an ink-stamped message on the back of each board with the manufacturing date and a reminder to "prime all your cuts." Bunt and his team changed the ink stamp to include a new message: CALL KURT FOR A SHIRT, with a toll-free number.

Kurt Williams is an inside-sales representative at the company, known for—among other things—his affinity for wearing a kilt. Williams is 50 percent salesperson, 25 percent customer champion, and 25 percent mascot. He was the perfect choice to be the "point man" for the T-shirt talk trigger.

To get their free shirt, customers saw the phone number on the back of the board and called Kurt. While on the phone to determine shipping address and shirt sizes, Kurt discussed new products with customers, yielding a tremendous increase in orders for specialty trims that many customers were not even aware were offered by WindsorONE.

"We'd send out extra shirts for the entire team. The goal behind it was to create downstream demand at the actual lumberyard, where the contractors are purchasing WindsorONE. Kurt would find out what lumberyard they were buying from, and also find out what jobs they had upcoming, and what products they might need for them," said Bunt in an interview.

One of the best elements of this program is that it became self-perpetuating as builders discovered it and told their friends and colleagues. Kurt would ask callers to take photos and send them to WindsorONE. Most builders would wait until their shirts arrived and then take photos on the jobsite. Bunt's team added those photos to the company's *Back of the Board* blog, which soared in visits to more than ten thousand per week.

WindsorONE Lumber CEO Craig Flynn explains how the program both made the company money and saved it money: "Instead of spending twenty or thirty thousand dollars on an advertisement, we're getting people to call us. They're calling us and getting a shirt and then we're saying, 'Oh, by the way, did you know we also make X? We also make Y. We also make Z.' These guys are running around telling their buddies, 'Hey, there's this Kurt guy. Call this eight-hundred number at WindsorONE. You get shirts.'"

Flynn says skepticism was thick at the beginning. Builders called the company, and they thought it was all a joke. "I mean, what company does this?" he asks.

The total number of potential WindsorONE customers is by no

means vast. There are only so many wood craftspeople in the United States, and far fewer work with the high-end specialty trims manufactured by WindsorONE. Despite this limited market, the Call Kurt for a Shirt talk trigger generated 18,752 phone calls from its inception in 2009 until it was paused in 2015 to experiment with a word-of-mouth program targeting lumberyard managers. The program is now back in action.

How many shirts does that represent? More than 150,000, including T-shirts distributed at trade shows, plus the Call Kurt program.

"We consider this pennies-on-the-dollar marketing because we simply added this little stamp on the back of the boards. So, if we're spending twenty-five thousand dollars on an ad and we get forty responses, versus somebody calling and then we send out shirts and catalogs and samples, the truth is we'd send it out either way. If somebody calls from an advertisement, you still need to get them samples. You still have to have a salesperson follow up with them, so the only thing that's actually different is the shirt gets them to tell their friends. Our cost per lead from advertising was something like four hundred dollars. Our cost per lead for this program is a free ink stamp and some shirts," Flynn explained.

WindsorONE used to rely on ads and product catalogs to generate demand. Indirectly, the shirts do the same thing, only better. Robbin Phillips and her coauthors would *love* WindsorONE. They wrote in *The Passion Conversation*: "Don't create brochures; create conversation tools. And keep in mind that less is more when it comes to these. Think about something as simple as a lowly T-shirt. Consider how a T-shirt with 'BREAK THE STIGMA' written on it invites a conversation. A hand-painted, one-of-a-kind Fitness Rebel T-shirt with your name on it invites a conversation. Less is more when it comes to stories as well. Short, sharable stories rule."

One of the secrets of Call Kurt for a Shirt is that the shirts themselves have talkable characteristics. They aren't just plain T-shirts festooned with the WindsorONE logo. What's the fun in that? Instead, they are interpretations of well-known logos and cultural memes, tweaked to be interesting to builders and craftspeople.

Says Bunt, "We want to make shirts that people are going to want to wear outside of just the jobsite, and that's gotten us a lot more play, too, because it's something that they'll actually wear when they're at home versus, 'Hey, I'm going to paint the house today. Let me put this cheap shirt on so I can throw it away once it's trashed.'"

Word of mouth works. It creates new customers, using conversation from current customers as fuel. But most companies do not yet have a strategy to purposefully create chatter. That's the difference between word of mouth and word-of-mouth marketing, and WindsorONE shows us how important that difference is.

You have a choice. Every business (and every person) has the same choice. You can try to be incrementally better than your competition and hope that customers notice it and actually say something, although they typically don't. Or you can embrace the "same is lame" philosophy, create a talk trigger like Kurt's shirts, and turn your customers into volunteer marketers, recruiting new customers through face-to-face and online recommendations.

But not just any idea qualifies as a talk trigger.

In our worldwide examination, we have uncovered the four criteria that need to be met for an operational differentiator to work as a talk trigger. We'll look at each criterion and some amazing examples of the businesses that embody them in section 2.

SECTION 2

The Four Talk
Triggers Criteria

e've discussed the importance of word of mouth. We've covered why it's so vital to actually have a strategy for creating conversation rather than just assuming that customers will talk about your business sufficiently. And we've seen why same is lame and how the power of true differentiation will spur chatter.

Now we'll dig deeper and examine precisely what is and what is not a talk trigger. Like Elvis, there are many talk trigger impersonators out there with wildly varying degrees of verisimilitude and effectiveness.

The remaining sections of this book outline our 4-5-6 system for building talk triggers.

In section 2, the 4 in our 4-5-6 system, we outline for you the four criteria that every differentiator needs to qualify as a talk trigger. Each of these criteria should be met, every time. Having this framework—a checklist of viability, if you will—makes it far easier to not only identify talk triggers in the wild but also to create your own when it's time to do so.

Not every differentiator can work. A cowboy who rides an ostrich is DIFFERENT, but does that quirk create downstream business advantages? Or is it just weird? In the immortal words of Spinal Tap, "It's such a fine line between stupid and clever."

Before we look at the criteria, however, we want to make sure you

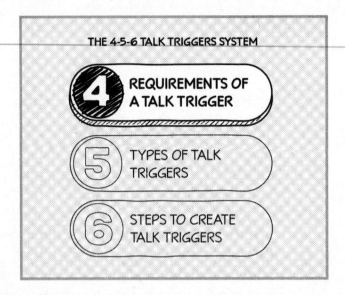

understand that there is no such thing as a universally beloved differentiator. There is no question that a true talk trigger creates word of mouth that brings in new customers. You've seen how that works for The Cheesecake Factory, DoubleTree by Hilton, and WindsorONE Lumber, and you'll meet many more businesspeople in this book who are propelling their companies with word of mouth.

But even the very best word-of-mouth strategies fall on a few deaf ears (or maybe it's mute tongues?). This is not necessarily because of the quality of the talk trigger, but rather the fact that some customers simply do *not* embrace different.

In our research work with Audience Audit, we asked respondents a series of questions about how much they notice and appreciate operational differences among companies. We asked them to agree or disagree with such statements as, "the best companies have something unique as part of their customer experience," and "the companies I support again and again offer something really different than their competitors," and "people look to me for advice about the best companies, products, and services."

After analyzing hundreds of responses and thousands of data

points, we found that customers naturally segment into four groups: uniqueness seekers, experience advisors, fundamentals fans, and skeptics.

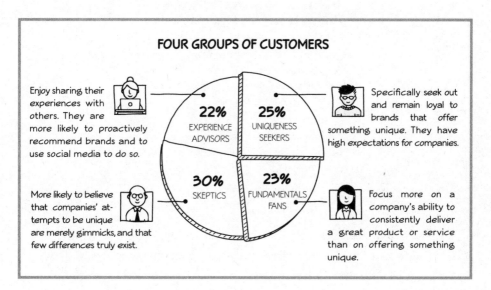

FOUR GROUPS OF CUSTOMERS

Enjoy sharing their experiences with others. They are more likely to proactively recommend brands and to use social media to do so.

22% EXPERIENCE ADVISORS

25% UNIQUENESS SEEKERS

Specifically seek out and remain loyal to brands that offer something unique. They have high expectations for companies.

30% SKEPTICS

23% FUNDAMENTALS FANS

More likely to believe that companies' attempts to be unique are merely gimmicks, and that few differences truly exist.

Focus more on a company's ability to consistently deliver a great product or service than on offering something unique.

Uniqueness seekers value, appreciate, and support companies that commit to doing something different.

This group shows no unusual age or gender characteristics. They just dig differentiation and want to talk about it. Sixty-one percent of this segment has proactively talked about The Cheesecake Factory or DoubleTree by Hilton, online or offline, and the chart below shows how much more uniqueness seekers value differentiators and embrace different as a business principle (answers are on a seven-point scale).

Experience advisors do not personally gravitate toward differentiators nearly as much as uniqueness seekers, but they are far more likely than the other groups to both talk about and ask about brands. They say they like it less, but they actually talk about it more. These are the people who are the most proactive about word of mouth, not necessarily because they love differentiators, but rather because it makes them feel good about themselves and their own expertise.

UNIQUENESS SEEKERS	STATEMENT	ALL RESPONDENTS
6.1	The best companies have something unique as part of their operations.	4.9
5.9	I tend to stick with companies who have something really different built in to how they do business.	4.7
5.6	I need a company to go above and beyond before I consider myself a fully satisfied customer.	4.6

STATEMENTS BASED ON 7-POINT SCALE.

Three-quarters of this group have proactively engaged in word of mouth, and the chart below shows just how much more this group wants to tell others about their experiences (again, on a seven-point scale).

EXPERIENCE ADVISORS	STATEMENT	ALL RESPONDENTS
6.3	I enjoy being asked about my experiences with companies, products, and services.	5.4
5.5	I often ask others for their recommendations before trying a new company, product, or service.	4.9
5.6	People look to me for advice about the best companies, products, and services.	4.6

STATEMENTS BASED ON 7-POINT SCALE.

Experience advisors are also far more likely to be female. Seventy-one percent of this segment is female, compared with fifty-three percent for uniqueness seekers.

Also noteworthy: Experience advisors are much younger than the other groups, with half of them age thirty-five years or younger—this willingness to express opinions, especially on social media, is a common trait of millennials.

Fundamentals fans are the lovers of USP (unique selling proposition). They care about quality customer experience more than uniqueness and are less likely to engage in word of mouth than the seekers or advisors. They prefer *good* to *different*. They also skew slightly older, with nearly half the category being age forty-five or older.

The last group, **skeptics,** is almost hostile to the notion of differentiators. They make up 30 percent of the combined customer base for The Cheesecake Factory and DoubleTree by Hilton and are almost twice as likely to agree with the following: "Usually when companies try to offer something unique, it's more of a gimmick than something that really improves my experience as a customer."

Even more pointedly, these talk trigger doubters are highly likely to concur with the following statement: "Companies should focus less on trying to be different or unique." Nearly six in ten skeptics are men.

Though a talk trigger strategy necessarily targets uniqueness seekers and experience advisors, don't discount the fundamentals fans and skeptics. As you'll see in the next chapter, although skeptics say they abhor different, that doesn't stop them from talking about your business. Whether they are seekers, advisors, fans, or skeptics (or your customer base is absolutely made up of all these segments), customers talk about you, both online and face-to-face.

The objective of a talk trigger is for that communication to be more consistent and compelling than it would be organically. Talk triggers make word of mouth purposeful and powerful instead of circumstantial and uncertain.

To do this, your operational differentiator needs to meet these four criteria. All talk triggers shall be: remarkable, relevant, reasonable, and repeatable.

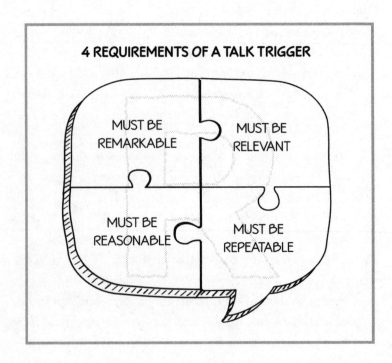

Let's look at the first criterion, perhaps the most fundamental and foundational of them all: the need to be remarkable.

CHAPTER 4

Be Remarkable

We see businesses conform to the pack constantly in our consulting work. Companies want to grow but believe that doing something different from others in their category is somehow antithetical to that mission, whereas the opposite is true.

Automotive companies miscalculate in this way all the time. "Let's make three vehicles that are ninety-five percent exactly the same, but we'll change the bumper and the lights, and the name. Presto! We have three new models, even though this required only a tiny bit of additional design and manufacturing effort." This fools no one.

Why do they do this? Often it's because they are trying to copy the competition. This is a self-limiting approach.

Harvard Business School professor Youngme Moon writes in her book *Different* that the business world creates conformity by creating competition: "Competition and conformity will always be fraternally linked, for the simple reason that a race can only be run if everyone is facing the same direction."

But it's not just the thirst to compete that squeezes the life out of opportunities to be different. It's also the widespread belief that operational competence alone is enough to spur chatter.

It's not. To be remarkable is the first criterion that a differentiator needs to meet to be a talk trigger candidate, and that means it's worthy of remark. It has to be a story worth telling. The Merriam-Webster definition of the word *remarkable* nails it: "worthy of being or likely to be noticed especially as being uncommon or extraordinary."

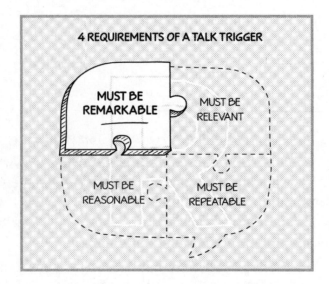

Remember, people rarely discuss adequate experiences. In the context of the word-of-mouth generation, *good* is a four-letter word. (Well, it's always a four-letter word, but you know what we mean.)

Yet even though every business on the entire planet has the same potential to be remarkable, very few choose to be different.

Maybe it's because being remarkable comes with the risk that you'll actually turn *off* a segment of your potential customers. Sometimes a differentiator is like a neck tattoo; it definitely stands out, but it's not universally appreciated.

For example, vegans aren't flocking to DoubleTree for a cookie they won't eat (although the brand is testing a vegan alternative for just that reason).

"Anytime you choose to take a different path, you are going to turn some people off. Their expectation was that this business was going to be like this, and if it is slightly outside of that, it's going to [be unappealing to] some people. But, one of the secrets to many successful brands is they have as many people dislike them as like them," says John Jantsch.

When it comes to talk triggers in particular, the skeptics may think your efforts to be remarkable are somehow disingenuous or frivolous.

What's amazing, however, is that in the survey these skeptics have recommended DoubleTree and The Cheesecake Factory *just as often* as customers who embraced differentiation. There is practically no difference between how likely a skeptic is to discuss a DoubleTree cookie or a giant menu from The Cheesecake Factory and how likely a nonskeptic is to do the same.

Being remarkable is so effective that it encourages people to talk about you even when those same people fervently believe being remarkable has no impact. This is like a Michael Jackson impersonator disavowing Michael Jackson as a stylistic influence; he may believe it to be true, but his behavior indicates otherwise. The chart below shows how often skeptics discuss the talk triggers of The Cheesecake Factory and DoubleTree hotels compared with the total customer base. Notice that their likelihood of doing so is essentially the same, whether unaided (asked, "What have you said about . . . ?") or aided ("Have you ever talked about the giant menu . . . ?").

SKEPTICS VERSUS ALL RESPONDENTS IN TOTAL CUSTOMER BASE

	SKEPTICS	TOTAL POPULATION
THE CHEESECAKE FACTORY MENU SIZE (UNAIDED)	33%	37%
THE CHEESECAKE FACTORY MENU SIZE (AIDED)	59%	57%
DOUBLETREE WARM COOKIE (UNAIDED)	35%	34%
DOUBLETREE WARM COOKIE (AIDED)	65%	69%

So don't be afraid of the skeptics. They might say that they don't like you, but they'll still talk about you—even when your product isn't flashy.

Retail banking, for example, is not typically a business category known for attention-grabbing differentiators. After all, most banks perform almost precisely the same function and are operated within a very narrow band of similarity. But Umpqua Bank is different. It has a talk trigger that compels conversation just by sitting quietly on a table.

Umpqua Bank

Umpqua Bank isn't afraid to stand out. In fact, it's part of its DNA. Founded in 1953, Umpqua is headquartered in Portland, Oregon, and has more than three hundred branch locations, making it one of America's fifty largest banking chains.

The brand began its drive to differentiate when former CEO Ray Davis arrived in 1994. Davis, a maverick banker from Atlanta, sought to reinvent the entire concept of a retail bank.

"For nearly twenty years we've been focused on creating a different banking experience, one centered on the idea that banks need to operate differently in order to remain relevant," said Davis in a 2013 article.

Entering Umpqua locations (the bank calls them "stores") is a markedly different experience. Not unlike your neighborhood Wal-Mart, each Umpqua store has a greeter that welcomes each customer or prospective customer and orients him or her to the premises. The entire store revolves around local businesses in the area: information walls; a retail center that sells neighborhood products; an interactive Discover Wall touchscreen that digitally showcases financial tools and product information along with videos by local artists.

As you might have guessed, many consumer banking customers don't visit physical locations as much as they once did. Umpqua counters this trend by turning a trip to the neighborhood Umpqua branch into an experience rather than an errand.

The most compelling in-store experience in each Umpqua location—the talk trigger—is a silver telephone. But it's not just any telephone. This special hotline enables any customer to press a single button to be connected directly to the bank president. Not the branch president, but the head of the entire Umpqua operation. That was Ray Davis until he moved to fill the role of executive chairman in 2017, succeeded as president and CEO by Cort O'Haver.

Tweets from the bank and its customers show just how valuable the hotline is.

Umpqua Bank
@umpquabank

Follow

What makes us unique? Each Umpqua Bank Store location has a telephone line you can use to call Ray Davis, CEO, directly-TeriLou

1:37 PM - 22 Jun 2009

Adrian Simpson
@AdieSimpson

Follow

At #Umpqua Bank any customer can walk up 2 silver phone in any of their 400 stores press 1 & speak 2 CEO. Amazing #CustomerExperience

1:13 AM - 28 Sep 2017

"Why hide from your customers?" asked Umpqua spokesperson Eve Callahan. "If you can be open and accessible, you should be. It's something we consider really important now more than ever. People are finding it more difficult to trust their bank and we want our customers' feedback, and we are here to answer those questions."

If he's at his desk, O'Haver answers the phone, often startling customers who press the button indicated just to see if it's authentic or a gimmick. It's authentic, and it creates conversation.

But don't think that you have to be a huge corporation to be different. In fact, it might be easier to be operationally different in a start-up operation, as Jay Sofer found.

Lockbusters

In 2008 Jay Sofer was an unemployed twenty-nine-year-old living in his mother's garage. Three years later he became the owner of the highest Yelp-rated locksmith company in all of New York City: Lockbusters.

Lockbusters' talk trigger created word of mouth on Yelp and elsewhere online and offline. Word-of-mouth referrals propelled his business upward quickly, assisted by the fact that many of his competitors are not particularly ethical.

"You don't have to go far in New York City to find someone who has been ripped off by a locksmith. The saddest call I get is from someone who said they recently had their locks changed but want to do it again because they don't trust the locksmith who did the job," Sofer told us.

Like Umpqua Bank, Lockbusters offers a customer experience that is meaningfully different from other locksmiths. For instance, the company provides guaranteed estimates; nights, weekends, and emergency service at posted rates; and flat-rate pricing on all locks and lock installation. Sofer's catalog of locks even features his own rating system (one to five locks) of penetrability.

It may seem obvious for a business to tell a customer the price in advance, but in the locksmith industry, it's exceedingly rare.

"A lot of locksmiths will charge you an arm and a leg, especially

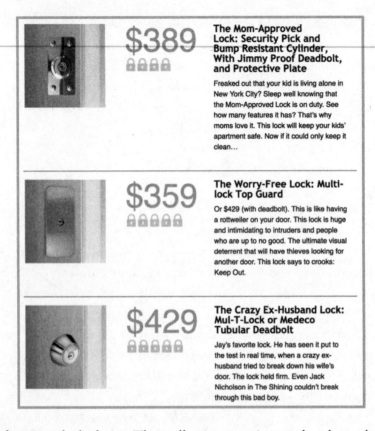

The Mom-Approved Lock: Security Pick and Bump Resistant Cylinder, With Jimmy Proof Deadbolt, and Protective Plate

$389

Freaked out that your kid is living alone in New York City? Sleep well knowing that the Mom-Approved Lock is on duty. See how many features it has? That's why moms love it. This lock will keep your kids' apartment safe. Now if it could only keep it clean...

The Worry-Free Lock: Multilock Top Guard

$359

Or $429 (with deadbolt). This is like having a rottweiler on your door. This lock is huge and intimidating to intruders and people who are up to no good. The ultimate visual deterrent that will have thieves looking for another door. This lock says to crooks: Keep Out.

The Crazy Ex-Husband Lock: Mul-T-Lock or Medeco Tubular Deadbolt

$429

Jay's favorite lock. He has seen it put to the test in real time, when a crazy ex-husband tried to break down his wife's door. The lock held firm. Even Jack Nicholson in The Shining couldn't break through this bad boy.

if you are locked out. They tell you one price on the phone, but when they get there the game changes, and suddenly you're paying more than you signed up for. That's not how we do it at Lockbusters. We don't take advantage of people in a jam—we name one fair price and stick to it. Period," writes Sofer on his website.

Sofer and his team also oil all locks for free—not just the lock(s) they service—and perform a security audit at every appointment.

The customer experience at Lockbusters is certainly enhanced. The way it handles its business isn't inherently a talk trigger; it's not remarkable enough to create a story. But Sofer's love of animals and complete commitment to animal welfare . . . That's a story.

When Sofer's beloved dog died, New York rescue shelter Sugar Mutts Rescue was the only organization that would accept his donation of used leashes, collars, bowls, and toys. This catalyzed a relationship that created a talk trigger that keeps Lockbusters' customers spreading the word.

"I'm fortunate that most customers have a good enough experience with me that they tip me, and tip me well," Sofer told us. "I quickly got to the point where I didn't need to rely on tips for my own expenses."

Sofer began donating a larger and larger share of his tips to Sugar Mutts. "I donate for selfish reasons: It makes me feel good," he says.

Lockbusters added a note about the tips donation program to its website, and Sofer began mentioning it to customers. A late-night emergency customer was delighted about her experience with Sofer and the donation program and wrote a blog post about it. That digital word of mouth was noticed by Wil Wheaton, a prominent actor starring on the hit television show *The Big Bang Theory*. Wheaton promoted the blog post on Twitter, and Sofer's Sugar Mutts talk trigger went viral.

Sofer's nearly four hundred five-star Yelp reviews are littered with extraordinary testimonials, including our favorite from Chantelle D. who wrote: "Is it weird I almost want to get locked out again so I can call Lockbusters? Yeah, my experience was that great."

Most of the reviews mention the Sugar Mutts program.

To increase the impact of his work with Sugar Mutts, Sofer recently founded the Keys to the Community, a nonprofit organization that functions as a charitable middleman.

Sofer is recruiting one hundred small New York City businesses and convincing each of them to donate ten dollars per month to collectively improve the city. The Keys to the Community bundles these contributions, and the participating companies determine where to direct the funds.

"It's just the right thing to do," he told us. "It's a cascade effect. If you do well, it creates good things downstream for everyone."

Being a great bank or an outstanding locksmith is a worthy

Sheila M.
Hastings-on-Hudson, NY
22 friends
11 reviews

Share review
Embed review
Compliment
Send message
Follow Sheila M.

★★★★★ 3/28/2017

After the worst ever locksmith experience, I just had the best ever locksmith experience.
If you live in NYC or the surrounding areas (Westchester included, obvs.) USE THIS COMPANY.

Jay contacted me within minutes of asking for a quote. Within an hour I had an appointment that worked with my weird schedule. He replaced my lock insanely fast. We chatted about the scam I'd just been through and what my options are as well as all the non-profit groups he's connected with over the years.

ALSO HE DONATES ALL HIS TIPS TO THE SUGAR MUTTS RESCUE. Jay has even offered to write a letter that I can send to my credit card company to help dispute the original locksmith charge. I feel like I can breathe again after dealing with a scammer for *a week* to get my lock fixed.

The. Best. Seriously.

objective—and should yield far better business outcomes than being a mediocre bank or locksmith. But to unlock the 19 percent of purchases that are directly caused by word of mouth, you have to transcend good and embrace remarkable.

Umpqua Bank's hotline phone and Lockbusters' donations of tips to Sugar Mutts are remarkable, which is why they are story-creating talk triggers and not just a nice feature.

But being remarkable isn't the only criterion for a differentiator to be a talk trigger. That differentiator also has to be relevant, as you'll discover in the next chapter.

CHAPTER 5

Be Relevant

What's the point of causing conversations among customers if that chatter doesn't tie back to your core business in some obvious way? Remember how DoubleTree by Hilton says the warm cookie upon arrival is a symbol of its commitment to hospitality? Or how WindsorONE's free T-shirts celebrate the importance of craftsmanship?

Many marketers overlook the importance of relevancy in their word-of-mouth programs and beyond. For instance, just about every B2B company, and especially those in technology, has launched some sort of contest for customers in the past. It's astounding that the prize awarded to the winner of those contests is almost invariably an iPad.

What follows is the entire list of companies that should give away an iPad as a prize:

- Apple
- Telephone companies
- Major electronics retailers

That's it. That's the list. If your company has *nothing* to do with iPads, why are you using your own time, money, and effort to create conversation around something that is manifestly unrelated to your own products and services?

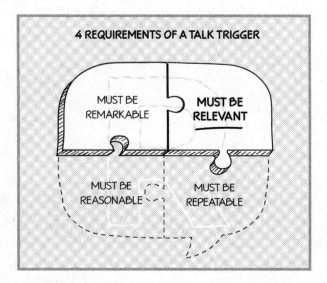

To be a differentiator, your talk trigger needs to be relevant. It should support your broader company positioning and objectives. It has to make sense within the context of what you do, who you are, and what you stand for. Let's look at how a family-run amusement park uses a hyper-relevant set of operational choices to create conversations while also improving the customer experience.

Holiday World and Splashin' Safari

Santa Claus, Indiana, is located ninety-three miles south of Jay
Baer's home. There are four things in Santa Claus; three of them are
corn. The fourth is Holiday World and Splashin' Safari, the world's
oldest family-owned amusement park and water park.

Founded by Evansville, Indiana, industrialist Louis Koch as a re-
tirement project in 1946, Holiday World has won a wheelbarrow
full of Golden Ticket awards (the Academy Awards of the theme
park industry) since inception, including Cleanest Park for seventeen years in a row.

The original catalyst for the park's construction was a mislead-
ing place-name. Koch was troubled that the village of Santa Claus,
Indiana, was a disappointment to children who found the environs
to be utterly devoid of St. Nicholas. First named Santa Claus Land,
the attraction included a toy shop, toy displays, themed children's
rides, and, of course, Santa himself. In 1984 the park expanded to
include Halloween and Fourth of July themes, and the name was
changed to Holiday World. The Splashin' Safari water park was
added in 1993.

Koch's Holiday World and Splashin' Safari have also won the
coveted international Liseberg Applause Award, which is given each
year to an amusement or theme park "whose management, operations, and creative accomplishments have inspired the industry with
their foresight, originality, and sound business development."

A commitment to operational excellence and customer experience is in the DNA at Holiday World and Splashin' Safari, and has
been for more than seventy years. But their talk trigger was created
in 2000, and it was developed because of a gut instinct.

The late Will Koch, son of the founder and president of the park
until his death, used to say, "When everybody else zigs, we zag." He

always issued that as a challenge, recalls Director of Communications Paula Werne. "What can we do differently that isn't the way everybody else does it?" Just because everybody else does it doesn't make it wrong, but what can we do differently that will get us that attention and endear us to people?

Matt Eckert began his career at Holiday World as the controller, responsible for finances. He's now the president and CEO. He remembers the genesis of the talk trigger quite clearly: "It was my very first day working here. Will came into my office and said, 'OK, I've got this crazy idea. I want to start giving away free soft drinks.' I looked at him—mind you, this is my boss—and I said, 'Are you stupid?'"

Eckert couldn't believe that his boss would willingly give away the nearly 100 percent profit margin on soft drinks. "But as Will explained it," Eckert says, "I became more energized by it, too, in terms of what this could do for our park [insofar as] differentiating us. It was (and is) something that no other place did, or does. The benefits that we've reaped from it are tremendous."

The amusement park industry was struck dumb by the move. Eckert saw it firsthand. "The first year we did it, when we went down to our trade show, people pretty much had the same reaction I initially had: They were coming up to us saying, 'Are you guys stupid? What are you doing? This is the craziest thing ever.'"

Werne says it was less confusion and more outright hostility. "They were angry. I think because they realized in their hearts that this was going to put our industry on its ear. I remember Will saying people he admired from other parks got in his face and expressed anger, 'This is the craziest . . .' Not admiringly crazy, but angrily, 'This is crazy. What are you doing? Why would you do this?'"

But do it they did, offering water, Gatorade, coffee, soda, iced tea, and more through 924 separate dispensers across the park. Drinks are also free at every restaurant on the premises.

The financial benefit of not having to purchase beverages for your entire family at an amusement park is sizable. In 2018, Six Flags amusement parks charged $14.99 for refillable soft-drink cups. But the advantage to Holiday World customers is more than cost savings, and the freebies create unexpected benefits for Holiday World as well.

"Back in 2000, pretty much all of our guest interactions were through comment cards and letters. Mostly, if people are going to take the time to do that, it's because they are unhappy. But once we launched free soft drinks, the petty complaints all but disappeared. They just didn't complain. And it's because they were hydrated, and feeling better overall."

Eckert agrees. "The number of first-aid reports went down dramatically that year because previously guests would go to the first-aid stations when they were feeling overheated."

The program also inadvertently saves the park money on waste disposal. "You go to a theme park and you buy a drink and then you want to get into the queues to ride an attraction and you don't have all your drink finished, so you just throw it away. So there's a lot of heavy, liquid waste that goes into trash cans," explains Eckert.

"The way that we have it set up, we have smaller-size cups at each of our dozens of Pepsi Oasis drink stations. Parents can go in and get their child a small drink and make sure that they have what they need, and that they're hydrated, but they're not getting more than what they need. So, we saw the amount of our waste go down dramatically as well."

Werne appreciates the intrafamily psychological advantages of free beverages. "I've always thought, too, one of the greatest things is Dad doesn't have to feel like a cheapskate. Isn't it nice to say to your kids, 'Help yourself. Take what you want. Mix up something; three or four different drink types' instead of, 'OK, we're going to buy one ten-dollar drink and everyone's going to have to share it.' Not to have to say no to your kids for one day is a wonderful thing for both parents, but I always feel like dads like it the most," she says.

Free beverages are a very effective talk trigger. This family-owned amusement park in rural southern Indiana has more than one thousand reviews on the TripAdvisor website that explicitly mention free drinks, including these examples:

⊚⊚⊚⊚⊚ Reviewed October 2, 2017

Great Value

I take a group every year the first weekend of Holiday World's fall pricing. The lines are short and the temp is usually pretty low. My group had a great time. Definitely recommend. They need more shade, but a great park. Free drinks!! Nothing more to say.
Show less

DaleS820
Cottontown,
Tennessee
☑224 ⚐108

⊚⊚⊚⊚⊚ Reviewed August 23, 2017

Lots of family fun!

Our kids (2&4) had a blast! They've been talking about it ever since. It was a good value compared to other parks and we never had to wait in long lines. The free drink stations were really nice too!

G1989DRhollyp
Huntsville,
United States
☑11 ⚐3

⚐ Thank G1989DRhollyp

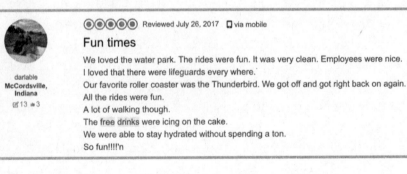

⊚⊚⊚⊚⊚ Reviewed July 26, 2017 📱 via mobile

Fun times

We loved the water park. The rides were fun. It was very clean. Employees were nice. I loved that there were lifeguards every where.
Our favorite roller coaster was the Thunderbird. We got off and got right back on again.
All the rides were fun.
A lot of walking though.
The free drinks were icing on the cake.
We were able to stay hydrated without spending a ton.
So fun!!!!'n

darlable
McCordsville,
Indiana
☑13 ⚐3

"Nearly everyone brings up the free drinks, even children," says Werne. The universal nature of the talk trigger helps, according to Eckert. "Not everybody's going to be a coaster rider. Not everybody's going to be a water park fan. But everybody's going to want to get something to drink when they're having fun and that's something that we give them."

The lost profit resulting from the program is substantial, but

Eckert believes the talk trigger more than pays for itself. Further, it's so embedded in the identity of Holiday World that it would be almost impossible to rescind.

Werne continues, "I remember so clearly the day we did it, sitting around the conference room table with the directors when we took the staff vote. I remember thinking, 'This is a moment I will always remember.'" She told them, "Remember, we can't take it back. This is a decision we can't take back. If we're going to do it, we have to commit to do it forever." And they did.

FreshBooks

FreshBooks is an accounting and invoicing software company for service-based entrepreneurs and small businesses. Many of its customers are self-employed, working in a wide range of industries, from plumbers and IT professionals to designers and accountants.

FreshBooks was a very small company at first, run from the basement of cofounder Mike McDerment's parents' house in Toronto. As the company grew, it chose to be cautious about spending money on travel to conferences and events, a mind-set it later realized that many of its customers shared.

By the time FreshBooks was large enough for McDerment to move the company to its own offices, he and his staff had begun investing in conference travel and event marketing. During one of his trips, McDerment thought it would be fun to email customers in his destination city, New York, to see if they'd like to get together for dinner. That idea turned into an entire program for the company. Indeed, even today, employees always seek out customers and have dinner as a group when they travel. Some of their customer dinners can be quite large, drawing more than one hundred business owners. It's always a FreshBooks employee who organizes the event, and it's always done at no cost to participating customers. It's a way to bring customers together and foster a strong sense of community.

McDerment likes the organic and free-form nature of the program. "They're kind of happening all the time; we don't even know about [all of] them. Sometimes FreshBookers [employees] will go on vacation. We've had people travel to Asia or South America, and while they're on vacation, they'll host a customer dinner in that area, which is, you know, crazy when you think about it."

One of the things that customer dinners do for FreshBooks is to help it connect business owners in the same community, which is an opportunity that not all small-business owners have. The experience of the dinners led FreshBooks to create a series of live, more produced events for its customers to help solve a problem its customers face. This series of live events, dubbed #IMakeALiving, takes place around North America. During these events, the company brings in authors, speakers, and experts to share insights with its customers, all for free.

The motivation for FreshBooks to create these events came from insights about its customers. Self-employed business owners tend not to travel much and don't always have enough time for professional development or personal growth. That resonated with CEO McDerment, as it mirrored his own experience in the early days of FreshBooks: "We . . . recognize it can actually be a pretty isolating experience. And so, what we wanted to do is create an experience where they would hear from other folks in a very honest and candid way about what's going on in their lives, because it's not all pretty. It's about an honest conversation around the realities of self-employment in this time and age, and it's an opportunity to come together and get your batteries recharged by hearing from others like you."

Attendees clearly value it:

In a way, the live events hosted by FreshBooks reflect the wonderful organic nature of its customer dinners, but in a more organized and scalable event. The events generate considerable word of mouth for FreshBooks, in addition to all the goodwill and happy memories. And it sets the company apart from its primary competitor, QuickBooks.

We've talked about the importance of being remarkable. We know through the great work of Holiday World and FreshBooks why talk triggers need also be relevant. The third criterion for a differentiator to be a talk trigger is for it to be reasonable. Let's examine this requirement next.

CHAPTER 6

Be Reasonable

Y ou get a car! You get a car! Everybody gets a car!"

With these words, exclaimed on September 13, 2004, television host Oprah Winfrey bestowed new Pontiac G6 sedans on 276 elated audience members gathered to watch her daytime talk show.

It's become an iconic moment and enduring meme. "You get a car" is part of American popular culture and used as a catchphrase, not unlike "Where's the Beef?" from Wendy's or "Whaaasssup?" from Budweiser.

Did Oprah's Pontiac giveaway (actually devised and funded from the marketing budget of General Motors, to launch the G6) create conversations? Of course. In fact, it ranks fourth on the list of all-time most memorable *Oprah* show moments, out of four thousand episodes, as ranked by Oprah herself. And how could it not? A car is an outsize reward for sitting in a studio audience and clapping when the APPLAUSE sign beckons. So much so, that it probably wouldn't work for you. Giving away 276 cars is big. Too big.

You're not Oprah. When Oprah gives away a few hundred vehicles, she can do so with nearly no skepticism created (although audience members were indeed shocked to have to pay up to $7,000 in taxes on their "free" Pontiacs). This is because Oprah has a deeper well of trust than almost any brand and has a pattern of giveaways and largesse. If Oprah said, "You all win a cloak of invisibility," nobody would question it.

Conversely, if you don't have that historical relationship with customers, prospects, and fans and you launch a differentiator that uses its scope and grandeur as the conversation-starter, you risk failure. Customers are suspicious when businesses promote something that seems too good to be true, because they've learned that it often is.

What does this mean? Your talk trigger has to be simple and reasonable. To "be reasonable" is the third criterion that needs to be present for a differentiator to be a talk trigger.

You're looking for the habitable "Goldilocks Zone," where the temperature is just right: a talk trigger that's remarkable enough to be a conversation catalyst but reasonable enough to be trusted. In an actual conversation, if someone hearing about your talk trigger says that "it's amazing," you're on the right track. Conversely, if he or she says that "no way; it can't be," you may have crossed the threshold into unreasonableness and doubt.

When you overpromise—or even when consumers simply perceive you to be overpromising—it not only depresses participation in the promotion or campaign at hand but also creates a longer-term spillover effect that diminishes brand trust into the future.

We want to underscore that every case study in this book meets this "reasonable" test. You don't have to spend a great deal of money

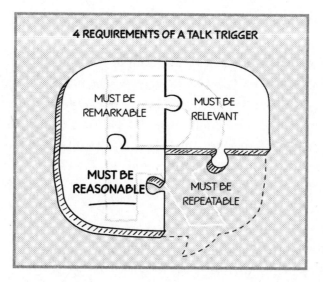

on your talk trigger—you don't have to be Oprah to get people talking! Of course, DoubleTree spends large sums on cookies each year, but it is giving away *millions* of them. The brand's investment in each cookie—the unit cost for word-of-mouth success—is exceedingly modest. Customers are not looking at the cookie and wondering, "What's the catch?" It's big enough to be noticeable, yet small enough to be trusted.

This is also true for one of the simplest, smartest talk triggers ever encountered. You'll discover it at another hospitality brand, Graduate Hotels.

Graduate Hotels

Graduate Hotels was founded in 2014. In just four years, the hotel chain has opened eleven locations and more are in the pipeline. Each

Graduate Hotel is situated adjacent to a major university, with a heavy concentration in "college town" metro areas with a large higher-education institution but a relatively small overall population.

For example, Jay Baer lives in Bloomington, Indiana (population: 86,000). Approximately 45,000 of those people, however, are Indiana University students and staff. It's a perfect city for a Graduate Hotel, and in fact, one is slated to open in Bloomington almost simultaneously with the launch of this book.

Graduate Hotels are located near the campuses of the universities of Georgia, Michigan, California–Berkeley, Virginia, Nebraska, and many more. Each property is enveloped in a heavy dose of local college nostalgia.

Every Graduate Hotel seeks to reflect the specific history, culture, traditions, norms, cuisine, and rituals of the nearby university. The carefully curated room interiors and public spaces feel a bit like stepping into a Wes Anderson film, but in a good way.

Inc. magazine bestowed a 2017 design award on the brand. How persnickety are the design touches? In the Berkeley location, the lobby includes a display of nine thousand vintage issues of *National Geographic,* chosen because the publication's signature yellow shade is an exact match for the university's team color. At the University of Virginia–themed location in Charlottesville, the floor of the hotel lobby is a tennis court, an homage to local legend and all-time tennis great Arthur Ashe.

Each of these little touches combine to create pastiche of the quirky, cool, and unusual. This is not an accident. "If it's obvious, we won't do it," says Ben Weprin, company founder.

That uniqueness cuts both ways, however. One of the word-of-mouth challenges of the brand is that each property is entirely different. Thus, while the tennis court creates chatter in Virginia, it doesn't have much talkable value elsewhere. Therefore, Graduate Hotels created a brandwide talk trigger that respects the local flavor of each destination, but does so consistently and realistically.

The talk trigger is the room key.

Unless you're staying at an old-timey inn that embraces the throwback charm of cut, metal keys, it's a near certainty that the next time you visit a hotel—including a Graduate Hotel—you'll be given a plastic key. These credit card–shaped access passes are inexpensive enough to be almost disposable.

Most plastic hotel keys have the brand logo on the front. Some hotels sell this space to local restaurants, such as pizza delivery. When large conferences are located in major hotels, the property often creates special, branded keycards with the event logo.

Graduate Hotels chose the remarkable option. The front of each keycard is printed to look like a student identification card of a famous alumnus of the nearby university. Brilliant!

The University of Georgia keys include IDs for sports broad-caster Ernie Johnson Jr., the longtime host of *Inside the NBA*, and NBA Hall of Fame inductee Dominique Wilkins, whose nickname in his playing days was "the Human Highlight Film."

Note that *Sports Illustrated* magazine tweeted about the keys last year. That will help your word-of-mouth propagation!

ESPN college basketball analyst Jay Bilas praised the keys on Twit-ter as well, noting that his keycard at the University of Mississippi–version of Graduate Hotels featured the ID of Cooper Manning (a former quarterback at the school and brother of NFL greats Peyton and Eli Manning). That's also not an accident, as Cooper Manning is now head of investor relations for AJ Capital Partners, which owns the hotel.

The keys have been mentioned in newspapers and websites dozens and dozens of times, and a large share of the hotel reviews on TripAdvisor mention the keycards as well.

Simple, reasonable, talkable. Graduate Hotels took something ubiquitous and mundane and turned it on its head. A great example of an operational difference that creates conversation.

But sometimes you don't even have to be different. You just have to be a tiny bit "more." That's the talk trigger of one of America's favorite burger and fries purveyors, Five Guys Enterprises.

Five Guys Enterprises

It was a choice that created a cult following.

Jerry and Janie Murrell told their four sons, "Start a business or go to college." The boys chose the former and opened a takeout hamburger restaurant in Arlington, Virginia, in 1986. By 2001 another brother had been born, and Five Guys Enterprises had opened five locations across the Washington, DC, metropolitan area.

Five Guys began franchising in 2003, and growth accelerated quickly. From 2006 to 2012, the chain grew by 796 percent, making it America's fastest-growing restaurant brand. In 2012 there were 1,039 restaurants open in the United States and Canada, with an equal number in development.

The chain excels because of its slavish devotion to customer experience, aided by a commitment to simple, repeatable operations and a dedication to being different.

Like many businesses with a talk trigger, Five Guys advertises very little. It spends the marketing savings on a sophisticated secret-shopper program that visits each location regularly to check for quality and process adherence.

Consistency in food and service is made easier by the fact that

Five Guys offers very few menu items and just one side dish: hand-cut french fries. They make it impossible for employees to serve a soft drink incorrectly, because every location has a Coca-Cola Freestyle machine, enabling guests to craft their own soda concoction. Further, beef and potatoes are never frozen, making it easier to cook them precisely and accurately.

Even though the brand is known for its burgers, Chad Murrell says fries may be more important because there is no do-it-yourself alternative. "You can cook your own burger in the backyard, but you can't make fries like ours unless you buy the best ingredients and practice our methods. It's a lot harder than just buying fresh potatoes." And Five Guys takes its potatoes very seriously; each restaurant features a sign that promotes the supplier and location of the current batch of spuds. It may seem a bit twee to name-check french fried potatoes like an urban bistro describes artisanal cheese suppliers, but fries are a BIG DEAL at Five Guys.

Sold in two varieties, salted and Cajun, the fries at Five Guys are generally understood to be outstanding.

But even if Five Guys french fries aren't your favorite fast-food tuber, just about everyone discusses the chain's talk trigger: Giving customers extra fries with their order.

Order a small serving of fries at Five Guys, and you receive enough fries to be credibly described as large. A medium order often solicits a "Wow, that's a lot of fries" comment. And a large serving

 Ryan Yoxtheimer
@yoxryan

Follow ⌄

The struggle of getting my burger out of the bag from Five Guys, due to the excessive amount of fries, is a struggle I'll never complain about

3:21 PM - 21 Nov 2017

of fries? Absurd, unless you're feeding a high school hockey team or a mining crew. Comments about the amount of fries routinely show up on Twitter.

The genius of this talk trigger is that the official portion sizes of the fries aren't larger than is customary or expected. Instead, the container in which a small order of fries is served is of normal proportions, but workers at Five Guys then add a heap of "bonus fries" on top. Consequently, when you open your sack of food (all orders, even eat-in, are all served in brown paper sacks to help execute this talk trigger) all you see are bits and pieces of burger-wrapping aluminum foil blanketed with french fries, top and bottom.

> **Christina M**
> @ChristinaMets15   (Follow) ⌄
>
> The best part about @Five_Guys is that they grab this tiny cup for 🍟 and then dump in fries 4x the amount that can fit in the cup
>
> 10:25 AM - 24 Nov 2017

> **Laura**
> @laura_allison99   (Follow) ⌄
>
> The amount of extra fries you always find at the bottom of the bag in five guys is what keeps me alive
>
> 3:38 PM - 16 Nov 2017

It's more art than science, but it's a consistent and reasonable talk trigger. Officially, workers are supposed to dump in a defined portion of bonus fries. But as a practical matter, that extra volume is often even more than that. It's just . . . a lot. All part of the differentiator, says Chad Murrell.

"I won't name names, but other restaurants just don't give a sat-isfying amount of fries," he says. "We always give an extra scoop. I say load 'em up and make sure they get their money's worth."

According to Murrell, some customers have qualms about get-ting *too many* fries. He says: "I just tell them to make hash browns with the leftovers. I teach my managers that if people aren't com-plaining, then you're not giving them enough fries."

Every hotel guest gets a key, and most patrons of hamburger res-taurants order fries. Yet Graduate Hotels and Five Guys made a choice. They chose to take a piece of their operational chain that most competitors consider mundane and unimportant and turn it into a talk trigger by making it distinctly, talkably different.

As Seth Godin wrote in *Purple Cow*, "Ask, 'why not?' Almost everything you don't do has no good reason for it." There is no good reason hotels don't create conversations through keycards and res-taurants don't through bonus fries. It's just not typically done. The brands profiled here asked "why not?" and reap the rewards of that inquiry every day.

These aren't grand gestures, however. The costs for the custom keycard is baked into the room rate, and the size of the fries (includ-ing bonus taters) is priced into the menu. These are not "you all get a car" moments; they are small, realistically accomplished tweaks that create big conversations.

But one of the most important components of the talk trigger at Graduate Hotels and Five Guys is that everyone can access them. All guests get a nifty keycard. Everyone who orders fries gets enough to build a raft. It's not a special offer, or a secret handshake, or a Sat-urday promotion. These talk triggers—like all talk triggers—are consistently applied.

That's the fourth condition that a differentiator needs to meet to be a talk trigger: It has to be repeatable. Let's investigate why and how that matters, including an example that's full of magic.

CHAPTER 7

Be Repeatable

Have you ever left something behind in a hotel and just resigned yourself to never seeing it again? When a young guest forgot to take his stuffed toy, Joshie the Giraffe, home from a stay at a Ritz-Carlton hotel, the staff made sure it got home. And they went above and beyond to give Joshie a grand adventure, including a trip to the spa, documenting the journey with cute photographs along the way. Maybe you've seen some of the many photos that went viral, or a similar story?

There's a trend in marketing, fueled by social media, of businesses trying to garner publicity by doing something special for a customer. Known as "surprise and delight" in the social media community, these initiatives typically involve finding a customer via Twitter or Facebook and then aligning operations to create a "magic moment" for that one customer in that single instance.

For example, author and entrepreneur Peter Shankman tweeted

that he wished he had a steak, and Morton's The Steakhouse brought him one, at the airport.

These heartwarming tales can create momentary spikes in brand chatter, especially on social media, where the sharing of poignancy (even if you are personally unconnected to the story) is seemingly a condition of use. They are also near-mandatory inclusions in every book, speech, one-act play, poem, and puppet show that is even tangentially related to customer experience, as models of how to treat your customers. Except for the one you are reading. Why? For a simple reason: Any differentiator that happens circumstantially is a publicity stunt, not a word-of-mouth strategy.

For every Joshie the Giraffe that gets spread around the internet like a regifted fruit cake, how many other surprise and delight efforts don't break through at all? A lot.

And even for those that do go viral, the lasting brand impact of these efforts is minimal. Although it may spawn some temporary goodwill for the brand, it quickly runs out of steam. While the story is cute, it's not personally relatable: It didn't happen to us, and we know it *will not* happen to us when we go to a Ritz-Carlton.

The problem with surprise and delight is that it's a surprise. It happens one time, to one person, in one scenario. That's not an operational choice that creates conversation day after day after day. Instead, it's one or more team members doing something special because they felt like it. A stuffed giraffe is a random act of kindness. A talk trigger is a strategic choice that you can implement every day.

A talk trigger should be offered to every customer, every time. The impact of that differentiator is far greater in total, because it is achievable by us all. We can personally experience it. It is a story in which we (or someone we know) are a major character.

Jake Sorofman, a vice president at the analyst firm Gartner, noted: "[I]n the game of customer experience . . . consistency will always trump delight."

We believe that not only does consistency trump delight but

inconsistency generates contempt among your customers (or at least has the potential for doing so). Nowhere is this more acute than in the airline boarding process. Airlines in the United States continue to add new "zones" such that loading passengers on an aircraft features laughably numerous striations. Presumably done to give frequent fliers succor and solace, having so many boarding groups (American Airlines currently has *nine* for every flight) cannot possibly be a great experience for fliers boarding toward the end, followed only by baby strollers, bags of ice, and assorted flotsam and jetsam.

Is the boarding process a talk trigger? Absolutely, and if you're in group nine, and it's not a happy story being told.

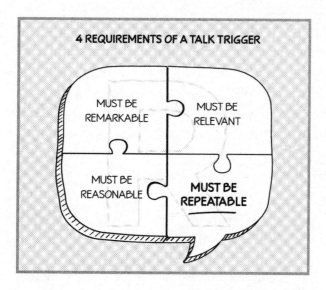

Robbin Phillips and her coauthors described the importance of consistency in *The Passion Conversation*: "The goal of any business should be to make word of mouth marketing operationally invisible. That is, it should be how a business does business not just one day, but every day."

To be a talk trigger, and to work for your business every day and not just one day, a differentiator has to be repeatable. It's not for randomly selected customers. Or your best customers. It's for all customers.

A business that epitomizes and encapsulates the repeatable nature of a talk trigger is the magician duo Penn & Teller. It's perhaps one of the more unexpected examples in this book. But perhaps that's not a surprise, as they specialize in the unexpected. Do you know their talk trigger?

Penn & Teller

Las Vegas, Nevada, is a city of magic. More than three hundred thirty working magicians are listed on the website GigSalad, and those are just the "call and get a magician for your party" variety of virtuoso. There are nearly twenty other more advanced practitioners crafting illusions in the city's bevy of casinos and nightclubs.

Penn & Teller stand out from this pack in several obvious ways. First, there are two of them: Penn Jillette, a tall and bombastic former juggler whose pugnacious public persona is used to present the magic in an unusually brash style. And the diminutive Raymond Teller, a sleight-of-hand master who never utters an audible word on stage.

Second, Jillette is quite funny, and occasionally edgy, and the mix of humor and magic woven throughout the performance is more suited for adult audiences.

Third, the duo have transcended the "magic show" career path, with several television series, books, and a Broadway show on their résumé.

Fourth, their consistency and longevity are astonishing. In 2014 Penn & Teller became the longest-running headlining act to play the same Las Vegas casino. Their show at the Rio hotel and casino began in 1993 and continues to this day.

But it's the fifth differentiator that truly makes Penn & Teller talkable. They've done it every single time, for more than six thousand performances. It's so simple yet exceedingly rare in the world of live entertainment.

The talk trigger for Penn & Teller? The performers meet their fans.

At the conclusion of each performance, the magicians dash up the center aisle of the theater, and as the house lights come up and the crowd of twelve hundred spectators files out, Penn & Teller wait in the foyer, ready to great each and every one of them.

They split up to increase their crowd coverage, and the magicians shake hands, take selfies, and answer questions until the last audience member leaves. Teller even chats with fans, which can be startling because few have heard him speak publicly.

Contrast this with other Las Vegas shows (magic or otherwise) that typically *forbid* photography of any kind, and if there is an opportunity to interact with the artist, that privilege requires a separate ticket and a hefty price tag.

"I still bristle a little bit at it being called a meet and greet because it's not organized, it's not charged for," Jillette told the *Los Angeles Times*. "It's just if you want to talk to us, talk to us. People [at other shows] pay a hundred bucks to go backstage," he pointed out.

Indeed, a meet and greet opportunity with large-scale illusionist David Copperfield after his show at the MGM Grand casino is priced at one hundred dollars and includes a handshake, autograph, and a photo that costs an additional forty dollars. Unsurprisingly, a review on TripAdvisor warns fans: "Do NOT purchase the meet and greet ticket," because Copperfield spends ten perfunctory seconds with each guest and tries to upsell additional pricey photographs and merchandise.

Even more than the low price of zero dollars, the most remarkable element of this talk trigger is that it is repeatable. No extra ticket is required. Every audience member can interact with the performers, and this confab takes place after every show. Not just on Saturdays. Not just during the holidays. EVERY show, for six thousand-plus consecutive performances. In contrast, the Copperfield meet and greet for one hundred dollars is offered only on Saturdays.

Each Penn & Teller performance and subsequent audience interaction creates chatter. There are thousands of photos and social media posts about these encounters, hundreds of reviews on websites, and dozens of blog posts. That's just the online word of mouth generated by this talk trigger. The offline conversation is also powerful. Jay Baer has seen the show twice and has told at least twenty-five people headed to Vegas about the Penn & Teller postshow hangout. And in contrast with Copperfield's reviews, online feedback consistently raves about the post-performance interaction.

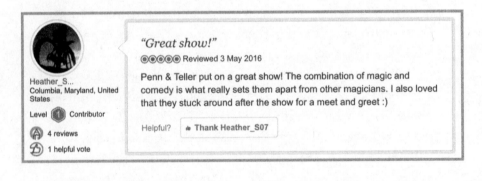

> **"Great show!"**
> ⊙⊙⊙⊙⊙ Reviewed 3 May 2016
>
> Penn & Teller put on a great show! The combination of magic and comedy is what really sets them apart from other magicians. I also loved that they stuck around after the show for a meet and greet :)
>
> Helpful?   👍 Thank Heather_S07
>
> Heather_S...
> Columbia, Maryland, United States
> Level 1 Contributor
> 4 reviews
> 1 helpful vote

Customers can certainly tell that Penn & Teller enjoy meeting them. Unlike Copperfield's perfunctory—and expensive!—handshakes and selfies, Penn & Teller take the time to really interact with fans.

Says Penn, "[We do it because] we love it. It started off when we were working at a theater in Philadelphia that had no backstage area. So the only place we could be before or after a show was in the lobby. And the audience would come out and talk to us. We just thought it was wonderful. . . . We have people absolutely from all over the world. It's really informal, there's no lineup. We bash out of the theater before the audience gets there, we stand around, they come up and do whatever they want. They want an autograph; I always have a Sharpie on me. If they want a photograph, I'm a master of the selfie."

"The real question is why doesn't everybody do this?" Teller asks. The real question, indeed.

Penn & Teller audiences get an autograph, selfie, and a heck of a story. Diners at Clube de Jornalistas in Lisbon, Portugal, get a story as well, but it's triggered by a very different yet repeatable gift.

Clube de Jornalistas

Clube de Jornalistas means "press club" in Portuguese, and it's a haven in the region. You don't need a membership or a secret passcode to eat at the restaurant portion, but Lisbon's Clube de Jornalistas does function as a journalists' club and serves many of the city's politicians, diplomats, writers, and business executives. Built in the eighteenth century, Clube de Jornalistas is a wonderfully charming restaurant, with a generous courtyard garden that provides an urban retreat for a quiet meal.

The setting is memorable as is the food. But as we've seen, operational excellence alone is rarely enough to cause conversation. After all, in a historic, bustling city like Lisbon, excellent restaurants of the charming variety are as common as Christina Aguilera costume changes. In Lisbon, "quaint" is table stakes.

Clube de Jornalistas takes a different approach to its talk trigger. Certainly, it works hard to deliver on the basics: excellent food, service, and atmosphere. It's ranked twentieth among 3,988 restaurants in all of Lisbon, according to TripAdvisor. But it also knows that word of mouth requires more than competency. It requires a catalyst.

"We believe that receiving guests is something special, from the way we welcome them, to the experience during the stay with us, to the moment they leave," said Luisa Torres Branco, co-owner of the restaurant.

Since the restaurant's founding, Chef Ivan Fernandes has devised little gifts to give patrons as they exit. A gesture to remember the restaurant and, hopefully, create conversation.

Fernandes's first attempt at a repeatable talk trigger was to give each guest a reusable cotton shopping bag. Branded with the restaurant's logo, this item had long-term value and spread visibility as guests made use of the bag during their errands around the city.

"The cotton bags revealed themselves as useful for our guests, especially due to the fact that most of them were traveling, and shopping was always in their plans," said Branco.

The next effort was to give each patron a luggage tag. This was a sound approach given that many diners at Clube de Jornalistas are frequent international travelers.

Both the cotton bags and the luggage tags are solid talk triggers but they didn't have quite as much talkability as the restaurant desired. They were useful gifts. And unexpected. But perhaps not unusual enough. The third talk trigger from the restaurant, however, unlocked the latent word-of-mouth power of its guests. All it took were some tiny fishes.

With some degree of frequency, guests ask for sardines at Clube de Jornalistas. It's not a particularly odd request, as sardines are incredibly popular among the Portuguese in summertime. So much so that during the country's Festival of Popular Saints in June, sardines are the official dish.

Despite their near ubiquity, sardines are not offered at Clube de Journalistas and never have been. The chef believes they are so ubiquitous that they are uninteresting in a restaurant setting. Upon learning that the restaurant was entirely sardineless, patrons are often dumbfounded or crestfallen. Branco recognized this disappointment and was able to apply a salve from the sea while also launching a new, powerful word-of-mouth device.

○○○○○ Reviewed March 12, 2016

First Dinner in Lisbon

Joseph S
Boston
☑10 ♦4

We walked over from Lapa 82, just a few blocks, and had one of the best meals ever. Codfish and octopus were wonderful, and the dessert, a mixture of sweets, was sinful. The owner, Louisa, and the staff were very friendly and accommodating. As a bonus, they gave us a can of sardines when we left!

Today, each guest at the restaurant leaves with his or her very own can of sardines. Diners who are sardine-averse can still opt for the luggage tag or cotton bag, but it's the sardines that create customer chatter.

You don't get sardines only if it's your birthday.

You don't get sardines only on your fifth visit.

You don't get sardines only if you spend one hundred euros.

You get sardines. Every. Single. Time. This differentiator is delivered to each guest.

And brilliantly, to reinforce the restaurants' "press club" theme, each sardine gift is wrapped up in pages of local magazines.

In this section, we've shown you the four requirements, or four *R*'s, that need to be fulfilled for a strategically developed operational differentiator to be a talk trigger. The differentiator has to be:

1. **Remarkable** and not just "good"
2. **Relevant** and tied to your core business
3. **Reasonable** and not so grand as to cause distrust among customers
4. **Repeatable** and available to every customer, every time

In the next section we'll discuss the five distinct types of talk triggers. These are the five conversational levers you can pull with your differentiator, and to understand how each works and how it fits (or doesn't fit) with your brand is key to effective talk trigger creation and word-of-mouth success.

Before we dive in, we'd love to know what you think at this point. Are you enjoying *Talk Triggers*? What questions can we answer for you? Take a minute to send us a note at JayAndDaniel@TalkTriggers.com, and we'll get back to you quickly.

SECTION 3

The Five Types of Talk Triggers

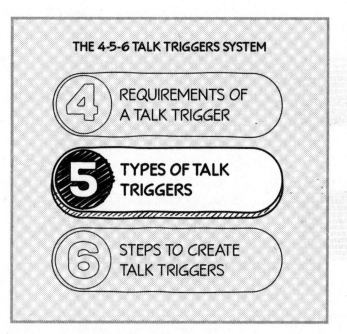

THE 4-5-6 TALK TRIGGERS SYSTEM

4 REQUIREMENTS OF A TALK TRIGGER

5 TYPES OF TALK TRIGGERS

6 STEPS TO CREATE TALK TRIGGERS

You've learned about the four criteria of a talk trigger, and you've seen examples of businesses of many sizes and types that are harnessing the power of customer conversations. Each of those examples met all four of the requirements presented in section 2. Every one is remarkable. They are also relevant. And reasonable. And repeatable.

But each of them, and the ten more you will discover in this section, also fits into one or more categories of the talk triggers typology. We developed this framework after studying hundreds of word-of-mouth examples and asking a seemingly simple (yet deceptively difficult) question: "Why do some word-of-mouth efforts succeed and others fail?" Put another way: "What is the commonality—the psychological binding agent—among the talk triggers that work?"

Remember: Word of mouth spreads when something occurs that customers do not reasonably expect. Customers do not expect soft drinks to be free at Holiday World, because they have learned over time that a Diet Pepsi is typically $162.75 in an amusement park setting. The gap between expectation and reality is the fuel for the stories that create word of mouth and in turn produce new customers.

When we dug deeper into what and when word of mouth works best, we realized that it's really about asking, Where can businesses most reliably exceed customer expectations powerfully enough that those customers are compelled to share their experiences?

After a lot of analysis and wrestling with taxonomy, we identified five types of talk triggers from which every business can select those that are the best fit with their operational and cultural realities.

The five types of talk triggers are: talkable empathy, talkable usefulness, talkable generosity, talkable speed, and talkable attitude.

Could you successfully introduce a change in your business that

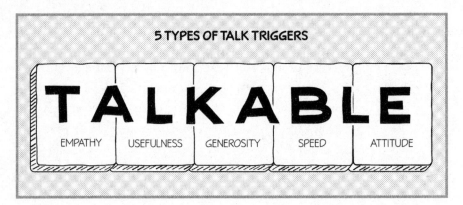

creates word of mouth reliably and does not fit into one of these five categories? Perhaps. But the overwhelming majority of talk triggers we have developed and studied fit into this model.

If we look again at the 4-5-6 system that forms the basis of this book, the noticeable differentiator that your customers will talk about has to meet *all four* of the criteria in section 2 to be a talk trigger. It needs to also fit into *at least* one of the categories in this section, and it almost assuredly will. This is especially true if you follow the six-step process for how to create a talk trigger that we will reveal in section 4, a few chapters down the road.

The five categories described in this section are very useful shorthand when talking about different generators of word of mouth, because they give you a rubric with which to compare and evaluate options and to increase your understanding of what works and why.

We gave a presentation recently at a large conference of tire retailers. One of the attendees has been unknowingly executing a talk trigger for twenty years. Before each customer picks up his or her vehicle after new tires are installed, an employee places a two-liter bottle of locally made root beer on the passenger seat with a handwritten thank-you note. This business is colloquially known in the region as "root beer tire."

A few dozen pages from now, when you experience a differentiator like that, you'll instantly be able to diagnose it as a talk trigger because it's remarkable, relevant, reasonable, and repeatable. And also because it's rooted in talkable generosity, with a side order of talkable attitude.

Recognizing these triggers in the wild is like spotting planes at the airport—your career as a word-of-mouth detective will open up all new fun and games for you. Let's begin.

CHAPTER 8

Talkable Empathy

As you begin to consider what your talk trigger could be, it's important to understand that all triggers fit into a limited number of archetypes. They all reside in one of five categories, and knowing this taxonomy will not only make it easier for you to identify triggers when you encounter them, but also will make it simpler for you to construct your own, using the six-step process we've developed in our consulting practice and will describe in chapters 13 through 18.

Each of the five types of talk triggers is talkable and will create distinct word-of-mouth advantages for your business, provided the differentiator meets the four requirements outlined in chapters 4 to 7 of this book. There is no "better" or "worse" type of talk trigger. Each is equally potent when applied consistently and appropriately. Certainly, some fit a particular corporate culture or

business category better than others, as you'll see in the next few
chapters. But all of them can work for you, if you choose to make
them work.

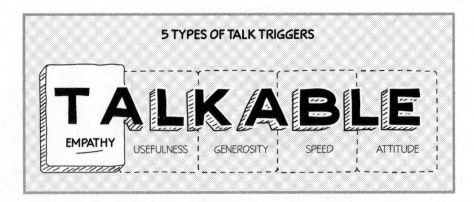

Let's look at the first type of talk trigger: using disproportionate,
unexpected empathy to delight customers and create conversations.

Empathy from business is in short supply. Shorter than ever perhaps, for two reasons.

First, empathy requires inconsistency. It requires listening. It
requires interacting with customers as a category of one. This approach, by definition, drives up the per-interaction cost of doing
business. In their zeal for efficiency and profits, most businesses
simply will not invest the time to deliver empathy.

Second, the human-powered approach inherent in empathetic interaction mandates that employees be given permission to work outside scripted boundaries. Some companies believe that this opens
them up to greater risk of crisis, or of legal action. In short, they are
afraid to be empathetic.

This is why, when businesses choose the opposite approach, their
empathy can have such a massive word-of-mouth impact. Even—
perhaps especially—when unfurled in an industry not exactly
known for empathy: overdue bill collections. Introducing: the talkable kindnesses of Americollect.

Americollect

In 1988, after being kicked out of college, a nearly penniless Kenlyn Gretz applied for a job as a bill collector at a five-person firm in Manitowoc, Wisconsin. He was given the job, making $4.25 per hour.

Twenty-nine years later, Gretz owns the firm, which now has 250 employees and is one of the largest and fastest-growing collection agencies in the United States. When Gretz bought Americollect in 1999, total annual revenue was approximately $600,000. In 2017? $25 million.

Their work can be unpleasant. It is the responsibility of the employees at Americollect to contact consumers who have unpaid balances owed to hospitals, physicians, and other health care services. The historical approach in the industry has been to push harder and harder, shaming the customer and using intimidation to extract payment.

Americollect takes an entirely different approach. So much so that its method of collections is woven into the DNA of the entire organization and is their unassailable talk trigger. The rallying cry of Americollect (it's even trademarked) is Ridiculously Nice Collections.

Wrap your head around that for a minute. The word *collections* goes with *ridiculously nice* like *Billy Ray Cyrus* goes with *New York Philharmonic*.

But it works. "We collect more money by being nice," Gretz told us. "We actually collect more money by being 'ridiculously nice' because consumers aren't afraid to talk to us.

"You see, a person's ability to pay changes. Just because they're a nonpayer today doesn't mean that they are a nonpayer forever. But we call them back a month later, two months later, three months later, and they take our phone calls, because we were nice to them the first time.

"But if you treat them like crap, make them feel like they're worthless because they don't have any money, they're not going to take your phone call the next time. That's how we collect more money: by simply being nice to them the first time, even if they don't have any money.

"One of the scripting lines that we train our staff to say is, 'You know, it sounds like you're struggling right now, but it certainly sounds like you're honest and if you had the money you'd pay it. Is that right?'"

Gretz says they've had multiple consumers say to his team members: "I wish my other collection agencies were as nice. Can I get my debt transferred to your office?"

Word of mouth among indebted consumers is, of course, limited. It's not a subject that most people are bringing up in conversation, even when stunned by Americollect's unusual approach. Among the hospitals and physicians that hire collection agencies, however, the "ridiculously nice" talk trigger is visceral and memorable.

Revenue Cycle Manager Deanna Christesen works for the Dickinson County Healthcare System, a ninety-six-bed rural hospital in Michigan's Upper Peninsula region. An Americollect client for seven years, Christesen confirms the "ridiculously nice" angle isn't just a marketing stunt.

"I have always been extremely impressed. They not only treat the patients that we refer to them ridiculously nice, but they treat us as a client ridiculously nice. Any communication I've ever had with them has been pleasant. So being nice isn't only passed on to the patient, but it's passed on to us as a client as well," she recalled.

"All the hospitals in the region network together, and I'm part of the revenue cycle group. I've actually recommended Americollect to several other hospitals, because their approach is so different and effective. I love working with them, and I've used some of what they've shown me to train my own employees."

Gretz says not only are there word-of-mouth benefits to being ridiculously nice, but the performance edge Christesen references is almost universal. Nearly every hospital uses at least two collection agencies, and Gretz says Americollect comes out on top in 95 percent of those comparisons. He says the firm has been defeated on performance three times in the past six years, out of more than two thousand clients.

"I would rather be nice, to consumers, than hit our financial goal every month. It's more important to be nice. And so, we focus on that. The money just kind of happens. You know what I mean?" asked Gretz.

Yes, we do.

The ability to effectively use an empathetic talk trigger isn't exclusive to the business side of health care, however. Physicians themselves can clone their customers. Dr. Glenn Gorab does so every day, or at least every Saturday.

Dr. Glenn Gorab

Oral surgery is, at best, a suboptimal way to spend an afternoon.

Uncertainty about the procedure is common. Concern about lingering pain is almost a given. Confusion about payment is typical, especially among patients without dental insurance.

Most oral surgeons and their staffs endeavor to answer these questions and quiet doubts when the patient is in the dental office. The best oral surgeons telephone patients the night after surgery to check on discomfort and residual bleeding and to confirm that postoperative instructions are being followed.

But then there is Dr. Glenn Gorab of Clifton, New Jersey, who initiated a talk trigger more than fifteen years ago, a differentiator that has yet to be copied by any of his competitors, despite its success as a word-of-mouth generator.

"I've actually mentioned this approach to several of my referring dentists, and none of them implemented it," Dr. Gorab told us.

What is this secret sauce employed by Dr. Gorab that no other dentist can or will deploy? Talkable empathy. Every weekend Dr. Gorab calls each patient that is coming to the office for the first time the following week. His typical greeting is as follows: "Hi, this is Dr. Gorab, I know we have an upcoming appointment for you next week. I just wanted to call to introduce myself and ask if you have any questions prior to your appointment."

This simple, remarkable gesture—connecting with a patient before he or she comes to the office instead of after—sets Dr. Gorab's oral surgery practice apart and attracts constant attention.

Dr. Gorab says patients aren't really sure what to make of the calls because they are so unexpected. "Most people are shocked that a doctor would call them prior to their appointment; they're almost dumbfounded. It's so out of the ordinary. They say: 'No one has ever done this for me before.'"

These patients tell their friends about Dr. Gorab's calls, and they deliver new patients through his front door on a consistent basis. His talk trigger clones his customers, as all viable talk triggers will.

"I had two new patients just this week who said: 'I understood from my friend that you were the guy that called her prior to the appointment, and I thought that was so nice I wanted to come see you.'" These patients drove out of their way to visit Dr. Gorab, bypassing dozens of highly reputable oral surgeons located closer to their homes.

Dr. Gorab says 80 percent of patients mention the calls once in the office for their appointments. "They say, 'Thank you so much for your call on Saturday.' Or, 'I'm sorry I wasn't home to take your call; thank you for leaving me a voicemail,'" he told us.

Perhaps the most interesting feature of Dr. Gorab's empathetic talk trigger is that it is so simple. Quite literally, every physician—every professional service provider, even—could mimic it, yet they do not. Why?

"I don't know why everybody doesn't do it, but I'm thinking it's they're either insecure or scared to talk to people about their service prior to meeting them in person, or they just don't want to be bothered on their weekend," he theorizes.

He finally convinced someone else to give it a try—a fishing buddy who is also a plastic surgeon. The friend immediately saw increases in patients and referrals.

And although it's not a word-of-mouth benefit, there is an important secondary advantage bestowed upon Dr. Gorab and other physicians that might choose to employ his system. Building empathy bridges with patients appears to generate goodwill that results in fewer legal proceedings.

Medicine is incredibly litigious in the United States and has been for decades. Ninety-nine percent of high-risk surgical specialists will face a patient lawsuit during their career.

Oral surgeons are similarly at risk for legal proceedings, but Dr. Gorab has avoided them entirely across his thirty-two-year career.

"I have never been sued for anything," he says. "And I do surgery; I do surgery every day. I have complications. Some of them have been bad complications. But probably the reason why I haven't been sued is because people understand that I care about them, and people don't sue people they like. The fact that I care about people is the biggest determinant of that, and the fact that I call them ahead of time means that I'm taking an interest in them and I care about them. So right from the start, they see that I care about them."

Among the five types of talk triggers, talkable empathy may be the least complicated to deliver and has extraordinary psychic and word-of-mouth impact. Next we'll look at an opposing, yet equally effective, form of conversation-starter, a differentiator that is talkably useful.

CHAPTER 9

Talkable Usefulness

Although being disproportionately empathetic works particularly well for Dr. Glenn Gorab, Americollect, and members of the pop band One Direction who are in touch with their feelings, other businesses and organizations just don't have the heart to use emotional intelligence as a talk trigger.

In those circumstances it might be rational to consider using a word-of-mouth engine that is, well, logical. Jay Baer wrote a book called *Youtility: Why Smart Marketing Is about Help, Not Hype* that showed how to grow your business by creating resources that potential customers find useful. This gambit can work as a talk trigger as well, provided you distill your Youtility down to its essence.

This talkably useful word-of-mouth propellant is particularly effective when put into practice in business categories not well known for making customers' lives easier. And we can probably all agree

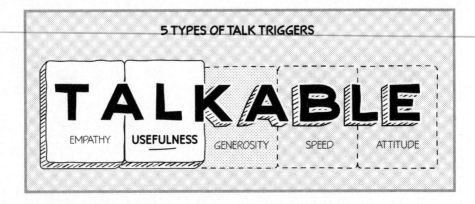

5 TYPES OF TALK TRIGGERS

TALKABLE

EMPATHY   USEFULNESS   GENEROSITY   SPEED   ATTITUDE

that the airline industry fits that pattern, which is why Air New Zealand's useful talk trigger creates so much conversation.

Air New Zealand

Based in Auckland, Air New Zealand is the official national air carrier for the country, flying to dozens of domestic and international destinations in nineteen nations. The airline has always operated with a bit of verve, as evidenced by its series of in-flight safety videos that turn that perfunctory bit of bored flight attendant theater into bizarre and delightful short films.

As ranked by the website Backpacker Guide NZ, these are among the top nine safety videos produced by Air New Zealand:

The Hobbit Safety Video: This video features characters and locations from *The Hobbit* film series, which were filmed in New Zealand.

The Bear Essentials of Safety: The central character is the madcap adventurer and fixture of any "best name of any television personality" list, Bear Grylls.

Mile-High Madness with Richard Simmons: This wacky exercise-video-meets-safety-instructions stars the cardio-fitness guru who dropped out of public view in 2014.

It's all wild and wonderful in an "I can't believe a major airline is spending a lot of money to be this outside the box" kind of way. To be sure, this is the *only* collection of airline safety videos that merits intentional viewing outside an aircraft, and even has its own You-Tube playlist.

You might reasonably expect these safety videos to be the Air New Zealand talk trigger, and you'd not be entirely incorrect. These mini masterpieces not only show you how to use a seatbelt in novel ways, but also they are so unusual that they definitely create conversation. But because they don't really benefit fliers in any meaningful way, and because it's fairly difficult to work "safety video" into a conversation with a friend, the word-of-mouth impact is slightly muted.

Air New Zealand's primary talk trigger is far more intrinsic to the product itself. At Air New Zealand, comfort is the driving force behind all facets of its product design, and it impacts every passenger, whether he or she is sitting in a spacious white-leather business class seat that turns into a comfy bed or in the last row of economy class, adjacent to the restroom.

While comfort is woven throughout multiple elements of the Air New Zealand experience, the true story-maker for the brand is its recently introduced redefinition of an airplane "seat": the Skycouch. The Skycouch is an entire row of three seats with movable armrests. Each seat also includes large footrests connected to the seat bottom. When the footrests are extended, and with the armrests removed, the whole row recombines like a midair Transformer to create a large, conjoined area that functions like a futon.

As described on the Air New Zealand website: "Imagine a row of

Economy seats that can be turned into a couch after takeoff. So you and your friend or family member can stretch out. Clever, right? Comfy, too. It's so flexible it can be used as seating, a couch or even a play area. You'll also get some lovely bedding and pillows. It's a world first."

The Skycouch changes how passengers think about air travel, because it changes what they can reasonably expect to do during air travel.

The Skycouch gives restless children space to spread out. It gives room for a couple to sprawl and relax on an overnight flight. Or, it gives a solo traveler a near-bed experience.

What's particularly interesting about the Skycouch is that it's a talk trigger that encourages conversation even if you don't experience it yourself. Just walking past a row of seats in the Skycouch configuration on an Air New Zealand jet is enough to cause a "wait, what is THAT?" moment and subsequent fusillade of questions and numerous tweets.

"What is really impressive is that Air New Zealand has continually innovated in the economy cabin, where most of us travel," said Geoffrey Thomas, editor in chief of the website AirlineRatings.

Air New Zealand is focused on giving customers something useful, whether they utilize it as a bed, a playground, or just an object of envy. The Skycouch talk trigger makes conversations appear out of thin air, even at high altitudes.

While Skycouch is an unusual feature of the core business for Air New Zealand, other companies take usefulness even further. Business-to-business software company Spiceworks, for instance, implements usefulness as a talk trigger so comprehensively that its entire economic model is unusual and unexpected.

Spiceworks

The software business can be extremely complicated. It can be tricky to know what features to build and how to package, price, and provision them. But the payments side of the industry is exceptionally straightforward. A company supplies the software, and a customer pays a monthly or annual fee in exchange for use of that software. It's like paying rent in Monopoly, but instead of "landing on Marvin Gardens," you cough up cash to "log in to your enterprise resource planning system." There is no free parking.

But way back in 2006—an epoch in software industry time—Austin, Texas–based Spiceworks determined that it would completely upend the established (and today, essentially calcified) protocol for software provision and use, and would instead give its software away for free.

"We've never sold software," Spiceworks cofounder and CEO Jay Hallberg told us. "From 2006 to 2010, Spiceworks was materially about free software for IT pros to manage their network, but we monetized by selling ads, instead of the software itself."

The impetus for the company was a realization by Hallberg and his cofounders about just how difficult the jobs of information technology professionals often were. "They didn't have a set of common tools to do their job. They didn't know where to turn for answers. They didn't know where to go to find people they could trust," Hallberg recalls. "We were blown away that in the three-trillion-dollar IT industry, there really wasn't a brand that was sticking up for the IT pro."

Spiceworks launched a small product suite that allowed IT pros to scan their computing network, monitor uptime, and track any issues or problems via a built-in digital help desk. The company built the first version of Spiceworks with an easy-to-use interface—and embedded advertising that paid the bills so that the software itself could be free to download and use.

"We thought about charging twenty dollars per month and being conventional," Hallberg says. "But we realized it was going to cost millions of dollars to get a lot of people to pay us twenty dollars per month, and what happened when someone came along with something similar and charged ten dollars?"

IT professionals used Spiceworks consistently to monitor the health of their network infrastructures. To provide this service, the Spiceworks software of course has to know what other software and hardware is present on the network. Hallberg and his partners knew that this knowledge gave the company an unparalleled ability to show hyper-relevant ads to Spiceworks users.

"We knew how valuable the audience was. The idea was this business could grow to global scale and could monetize it in an interesting way and scale faster than if we were ever to charge for the software. And we'd be doing an incredible service while we're at it and helping IT pros learn about the products and services they need."

Spiceworks was different—and even the ads were useful, because they were so tailored and targeted.

Shortly after launch, Spiceworks began to understand that the collaboration and community needs of IT professionals superseded even its need for network monitoring software. In an effort to solicit feedback from early users, Hallberg and his associates created a web page where customers could submit ideas for features to include and could vote them up or down based on interest.

Using the "Spiceworks theme," each vote took the form of an on-screen chili pepper, and soon IT pros were "spicing up" or "spicing down" ideas with regularity. What began as a relatively simple voting mechanism soon expanded to become an online support group.

"They started talking to each other about how to solve problems with Spiceworks," says Hallberg. "Somebody wrote, 'Hey, I can't get Spiceworks to talk to this device.' Somebody else would answer, 'I had that same problem. Here's how I fixed it,' or, 'I talked to the Spiceworks engineers about it. Here's what they did.'"

These conversations steadily expanded and morphed until, in 2008, participants began asking questions about topics other than Spiceworks itself. Like what kind of router to buy. Or, how to ask a boss for a raise.

"When we saw that, we knew we really might be onto something here," Hallberg remembers.

Certainly, IT professionals had other places to ask questions and interact online, even back in 2008. But essentially all the other options were topically narrow and vendor specific. Cisco had a forum for Cisco customers to ask Cisco questions, for example. But Spiceworks was the first—and now by far the most popular—online destination for the IT world to ask questions and interact on just about any subject.

Recognizing this as an incredibly useful resource, Spiceworks opened up the online community to noncustomers in 2010. "That's when the word of mouth kicked in," says Hallberg. "Because that's when people would tell their friends about what a great place Spiceworks was and if you're in IT, you need to go there. But then as that community content grew, Google started finding it, too, and as other people had the same questions, Spiceworks would increasingly show up in Google search results.

"We had kind of stumbled into being a place for people who were IT generalists, each of whom had to know a lot about a lot. We built this collegial, collaborative, vendor neutral community that was about people who did this particular thing for a living, first and foremost."

In 2018 the Spiceworks community is extraordinarily passionate and connected, online and offline. The online destination is visited by more than seven million people each month. Spiceworld, the annual Spiceworks conference, is like the world's nerdiest tent revival. It's pretty much what you would expect if you put two thousand people in a room who all happened to be conversant in network architecture and then plied them with bacon and beer (the unofficial talismans of Spiceworks members).

In 2016 Hallberg and his team embarked on what it internally called "chapter three"—an initiative to become *the* single, unified source of information, education, and interaction for IT professionals worldwide. This entails the creation of new content management and machine learning systems to empower the community and give each member a massively customized view of all things IT.

Hallberg says Spiceworks has four objectives: "One, connect them to the right people and content to do their job, whether that's solve a problem or work on the next big thing. Two, help to finish the project they're on or get their next job. Three, help them find and buy the right products and services they need for business. And four, give them the tools that they need to get their job done."

It works. The Spiceworks brand is to the IT community as retro eyeglasses are to the hipster community: a popular and powerful sign of inclusion that creates conversation by being massively useful to its members.

Spiceworks member Alan Boushard perhaps wrote it best in this ode to Spiceworks, posted on Valentine's Day 2015:

How do I love thee? Let me count the ways.

I love thee to the depth and breadth of the community's knowledge base.

For when I have a strange problem they are always there with an answer.

I love thee for the insight into bacon, beer and anything technology based.

For when I implement a new solution, I have reviews, how-tos that will guide me along my way.

I love thee for the friendship of the community.

For when I need advice they never disappoint with sound judgment and encouragement along the way.

I love thee for the training that is offered.

For when I am stuck in a bad position I can improve myself for that dream position.

I love thee for Spiceworld and all the fun that is had.

For when I attend I get free bacon and beer, nuff said.

Sometimes the best talk triggers just require you to have an exceptionally strong sense of what your customers and potential customers really want. Then you just give that to them in a way that's remarkable, consistent, reasonable, and talkable.

If you're sick of being cramped in economy airline seats, and you're frazzled by your kids bouncing around on a transcontinental flight like 1920s teens doing the Charleston, what you really want—and what you'll definitely talk about—is a Skycouch.

If you're exhausted by trying to keep up with the constant changes in your field, you need a hand deciding what to buy and when, and you desperately need some colleagues who know just how frustrating it is that Phil in accounting still can't figure out how to use Microsoft Excel, what you really want—and what you'll definitely talk about—is the Spiceworks community.

As a talk trigger, usefulness can absolutely be an effective option. But it's not the only choice. In fact, some businesses create consistent customer chatter by giving customers more than they expected. This is the generosity approach, and it's one of the strongest of the five types of talk triggers.

CHAPTER 10

Talkable Generosity

When portions get smaller but prices stay the same, the effect is a hidden price increase called "shrinkflation." We are surrounded by it.

According to a study by the Office for National Statistics in the United Kingdom, 2,529 separate products decreased in size between 2012 and 2017. From a bag of Doritos containing fewer chips to airlines charging fees for every conceivable option, consumers are besieged by companies giving them less for the same price, or worse yet, less for a higher price.

We all know this to be true. We all feel it. And the omnipresence of shrinkflation is why talk triggers that do the opposite are so effective. This is the power of generosity.

You've learned about other talk triggers that utilize generosity elsewhere in this book. Free beverages at Holiday World? That's a generosity trigger. Customers create conversations about it because

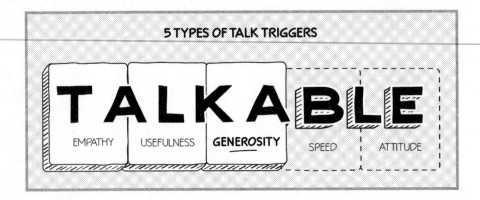

they are stunned that a company would forgo the profit potential and just give drinks away, gratis. The extra fries in the bag at Five Guys? Also a generosity trigger.

But nothing—and we mean *nothing*—causes conversation like a flamingo strutting by when you're attending a conference. This latest talk trigger commenced in 2016, and it can be experienced at the Flanders Meeting & Convention Center Antwerp in Belgium.

Flanders Meeting & Convention Center Antwerp

Opened in 1843, Antwerp ZOO is the oldest public scientific zoo in the world. In the nineteenth century, zoos had a very strong social function and the animals were not the central attraction, according to Anja Stas, chief commercial officer for the Flanders Meeting & Convention Center Antwerp. This means there's always been the need for a multitude of entertaining spaces to complement the scientific zoo, and the first marble ballroom opened way back in 1897.

More than three hundred events per year are staged at the facility. This high demand presented a strong argument to get bigger and more talkable. Working with the city of Antwerp, management sought to create a larger, more modern international convention center to capitalize on the city's central location and transportation hub.

"In talking with the city, it became clear that it was an incredible opportunity to—instead of remodeling—rebuild the existing concert hall from scratch within the historic wing of the facility. And also to build an extra thirty meeting rooms to make it a complete, fully purpose-built, ultrainternational convention center," says Stas.

The rebuilt Queen Elizabeth Hall opened in November 2016. Because Stas and her colleagues already ran events (plus a large zoo), the newly expanded meetings center instantly had a sales team, marketing team, guest relations team, and other functions. From an operations and financial perspective, the new Flanders Meeting & Convention Center Antwerp made a tremendous amount of sense.

But those benefits don't particularly resonate with event attendees and other users of the facility. To get them talking, Stas had to create something more: a generosity talk trigger.

Each and every attendee at the convention center gets completely free, unlimited access to the zoo for the duration of their event. Come for the convention, stay for the koalas! Zoo admission is twenty-six euros per day, so the ability of conferencegoers to visit as much and as long as they like is potentially a significant financial savings.

The facility team also works with each group to weave the zoo into the agenda, whether it's a coffee break with penguins or dinner in the aquarium. Meeting attendees even get special early-morning access to the zoo for strolls or jogs before the gates are opened to the public. "For me, it's the most magical hour in the zoo. It's the hour when the animals wake," says Stas.

And for companies or associations with stated corporate social responsibility (CSR) goals, those CSR objectives can at least partially be met just by locating a meeting or conference at the facility. This is because 100 percent of event proceeds fund animal conservation efforts managed by the Antwerp ZOO Foundation.

Among meeting planners all over the world, Flanders Meeting & Convention Center Antwerp is now known as A Room with a ZOO.

So recognized is this talk trigger that Stas and her team won the prestigious International Congress and Convention Association Best Marketing Award in 2017, recognizing the world's best program to promote a destination or facility. The comparatively tiny A Room with a ZOO bested the $2 billion International Convention Centre Sydney in the final round of peer judging.

Says Stas: "I was trained at Coca-Cola, so I know a bit about building brands and emotional storytelling. When I entered this industry three years ago, what I noticed was that marketing was pretty conventional and traditional in this industry . . . destinations sometimes don't go far enough in really building bridges to their audience and finding those triggers that really move people and engage them on an emotional level. Because that's the only way to truly make a difference and to stand out."

And just like when Holiday World began offering free soft drinks, industry experts and competitors scoffed at the concept. "They said: 'You're not going to be taken seriously,'" Stas remembers. "A zoo with a convention center, that's not serious."

She pressed onward, regardless. "It actually makes meetings not just more fun, but science has proven that having nature and animals present during your meeting actually makes the meeting more effective."

And, a *lot* more talkable.

Stas gave a presentation to international meeting planners recently, and a follow-up survey found that 100 percent of attendees were interested in learning more about A Room with a ZOO.

The presence of giraffes, gorillas, elephants, an aquarium, and hundreds of other animals adjacent to your conference space provides some fantastic social media opportunities as well, further spreading the message that things are decidedly different in Antwerp.

Certainly, if you have access to a zoo, you should strongly consider building a talk trigger around it. Realistically, most of us can't do that. But all of us can do something different in our own way. Welcome to Skip's Kitchen in Sacramento, California, where playing cards are the key to a most delightful talk trigger.

Skip's Kitchen

For seventeen years, Skip Wahl worked his way up the ranks at Brinker International Restaurants, owner of the Chili's chain, among others. At his peak, Wahl was managing partner of one of the busiest Chili's locations in Northern California.

"It was a lot of fun," he recalls. "But I was not necessarily a rule follower. I was more of a rule challenger. I was the guy always raising his hand in meetings and asking why," says Wahl.

"That limited my chances for advancement, and after a lot of research and conversations with my wife, we decided in 2010 to open our own spot in Sacramento."

Skip's Kitchen is a simple affair, with a concise menu (think of it as the anti–Cheesecake Factory) featuring outstanding hamburgers, great fries, a few interesting appetizers, and a lot of fun twists. How good are the burgers? Skip's Kitchen was named America's twenty-ninth best hamburger purveyor in 2017.

Since the day his restaurant opened on October 10, 2011, Wahl has spent a grand total of zero on advertising and marketing. Certainly, great burgers help. As does Wahl and his wife's commitment to the local community and warm and inviting customer service.

But because it's difficult to have food quality and service quality that are so off the scale that they register as *remarkable* and *talkable*, other characteristics have to do the heavy lifting instead when it comes to generating word of mouth. In fact, 2016 research from Nur A'mirah Hassan Basri and collaborators found that the quality and uniqueness of a restaurant's physical environment are the most important factors in influencing dining choices, and the least important factor is food quality.

The success of Skip's Kitchen reflects those insights. The restaurant has a remarkably generous talk trigger that also creates an electric physical environment. The creation and adoption process of this differentiator was equal parts intuition and necessity.

The necessity part came from the problem of tracking customers' orders. Wahl at first just tried to remember what each of his nine tables had ordered at the counter, but that got confusing on the first day. He then considered using plastic numbers that guests would prop up on their table, similar to how Carl's Jr. and Hardee's restaurants deliver orders. But he wanted to do something more visually interesting, so he thought, *Let's just use a deck of cards.*

"People come in and order and we'd give them a card, and they'd get the three of clubs or something. So we write that down on their ticket, and when the food comes up, we deliver it to the one with the three of clubs on the table," Wahl explained.

But Wahl didn't just want to make food delivery more organized. He wanted a hook. "It's a small place. Not that much room. So when it's busy, the line can be out the door, and that was starting to actually hurt business," Wahl remembers. "There's this old saying by Yogi Berra: 'Nobody goes there anymore. It's too crowded.' That was becoming a problem for us."

Needing a mechanism to keep patrons standing patiently in line, he first pondered installing outdoor televisions but then hit upon a superior idea that creates much better stories.

"It was a Friday morning and two ladies in their midseventies came in and ordered two Asian salads with chicken, and I said, 'Ladies, I'm going to try something here,'" Wahl remembers. "'I'm going to fan out these playing cards facedown, and if you pick the joker, your entire meal is free.'

"One of them picked a card and *boom*, she picked the joker. First time out of the chute, a winner! And I said, 'This may be a terrible and expensive idea!'"

But Wahl persisted for the remainder of the day, and customers loved the chance to win. So he tried it again the next day. And the next.

"People's eyes started lighting up, and they jockeyed for position in the line to be able to see the customers in front of them try it. When they came in groups, while in line, they started talking about who was going to pick the card," he recalls.

"From a business perspective, the better way to do it would be to pay for half of your order. Or, to give you a gift card. But it just didn't have the right ring to it. It's much stronger to say to every guest, 'You pick the joker, I'm buying your meal.'"

On average, four customers win every day, meaning Wahl gives away approximately 2 percent of his orders. But when they win, the talk trigger pays off repeatedly. Lucky patrons take selfies, post to Facebook, write reviews, and tell their friends.

Ashley T.
Sacramento, CA
👥 **304** friends
⭐ **68 reviews**
📷 **23 photos**

Share review
Embed review
Compliment
Send message

⭐⭐⭐⭐⭐ 10/17/2017

Friendly staff, cute lobby, and when you order food they do this magic trick where they flair out a deck of cards and if you chose the joker meals on them! Didn't win but was still fun! And the card you chose is your number! Super creative!

Food was great simple menu but a lot of choices which is nice!

Had pesto chicken added bacon it was great!

kyrabob42
Local Guide · 1 review
★★★★★ 2 months ago

Good food, awesome atmosphere and if you get lucky you can get your meal for free! If you pick the joker from their deck of cards, they'll pay for your meal, and they do follow through on this. My husband and I got our meals and a milkshake for free today!

Kim Poulsen-Smith reviewed Skip's Kitchen — 🌀   ···
August 7 · 🌐

So good. Always consistent. Served fresh and the staff is alway a happy bunch. We shared the Mac and cheese balls. I had the Chinese salad and hubby had the bacon cheese burger with criss cross fries. We will be back with the hopes of finding that Joker.

Even though it costs more in free food, from a word-of-mouth perspective it's better for Wahl when larger groups of customers pull the joker. The biggest bill he's had to cover was $117.86, when a group of ten hungry Eagle Scouts ordered many, many burgers.

"The last kid to order I knew from around town. His name is Christian," recalled Wahl. "He ordered his burger and he said, 'And I'm going to pick the joker and it's right there.' And he turned the card over and *boom*, it was right there. They all ran around the restaurant like they just won the Super Bowl! The whole place was clapping and high-fiving them. And when they went home, guess what they told their parents? 'I hit the joker.' And it creates return business."

The joker at Skip's Kitchen is so well known now that some Sacramento residents don't even know the name of the restaurant—but they know the talk trigger.

The "card trick" is so popular that Skip's Kitchen diners occasionally try to game the system. When the nine-table restaurant is packed, nine cards are out of the deck at the tables, raising the odds of winning from one in fifty-three to one in forty-four. Guests will sometimes "graciously" allow others to cut in line in front of them, purposefully delaying their own orders until the odds improve.

Frequent customers often bring Wahl souvenir decks of cards from their travels, which he proudly displays near the Skip's Kitchen T-shirts. Amazingly, the shirts are not for sale. You can only get one if your name is also Skip; if it is, the shirt is free. Thirteen have been redeemed.

Consumers are so accustomed to constantly getting less that giving them just a little bit more (or at least a chance to get more, like at Skip's Kitchen) can be enough to get them telling your story and igniting word of mouth. But some organizations are unwilling or unable to use largesse as a talk trigger.

Instead, they rely on nimbleness to shock their customers and fans into proactive conversations. Like Taylor Swift changing musical genres, these talk triggers are talkably fast. Let's take a look at how they do it.

CHAPTER 11

Talkable Speed

S peed matters. In fact, 41 percent of consumers say that when they contact a business, "getting my issue resolved quickly" is the most important element of a good customer experience. In that survey, speed was rated 350 percent more important than "politeness of the company representative."

Further, more than nine in ten American consumers say they refuse to wait on hold for more than five minutes when calling a business. This finding, of course, makes us wonder about the other 10 percent who have nothing better to do than listen through a phone speaker to Kenny G and the other smoooooth jazz greats that make up the typical "on hold" playlist.

What's insidious about consumers' need for speed, however, is that it's a constantly moving target. What was considered fast in 2010 is table stakes today. What was considered fast in 2000 is now slow. And what was considered fast in 1990 is now akin to churning your own butter while listening to Glenn Miller's big band on your dad's record player.

In three decades or so, we moved from fax to overnight delivery to email to instant and text messaging to Netflix and "instant everything" via mobile app. At this rate, telepathy is just around the corner. And speed is only one element of consumers' changing expectations. Simply making things faster at the expense of some other element of your customer experience is not a talk trigger.

But speed is unique in its relentlessness. Making sure a restaurant has "good food" has always been important, but the bar to clear for the food to be "good" hasn't inched up every year. For a company to be fast enough to be talkable is an exceptionally high standard today, which is why it's operationally difficult to create a speed-based talk trigger. Speed is a moving target that you will consistently need to invest to protect the remarkability of your talk trigger. That said, for companies that decide to own this part of customer experience and remain committed to it, speed can pay off like a rigged slot machine.

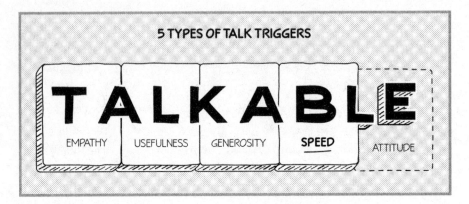

Paragon Direct

"Why is Amazon doing better in the retail space than Google? Because Google brings the customer to the product, and Amazon brings the product to the customer," says Brian Benstock, a thirty-five-year veteran of the automotive industry.

In an interview, Benstock reminded us that although Google is the number one search engine overall in the United States, Amazon is by far and away the number one search engine when consumers are looking to purchase a product, because it offers the most frictionless experience. The distance between desire and fulfillment is shorter using Amazon than just about anywhere else, and that's what Benstock is trying to bring to auto service. The nucleus of his talk trigger? Making a clunky service experience feel like a seamless retail experience.

Benstock is VP and general manager of Paragon, the number one seller of certified, preowned Honda and Acura vehicles in America.

One of the secrets to his success is his understanding that many of the historical norms in the industry are convenient for dealers but markedly less so for customers. How have auto retailers been able to whistle through the graveyard of increasing customer expectations? By the grace of the virtual monopolies they are bestowed via franchise agreements with manufacturers.

Dealership service departments often close at five or six o'clock in the evening, and many are not open on the weekends. This has spawned an entire industry of service competitors like Jiffy Lube, Meineke, and Pep Boys.

"Dealership service hours are convenient for nobody except for the dealer," Benstock asserts.

"The franchise system that was designed to protect the dealers has actually been creating incredible opportunities for competitors to feed off of the dealerships' poor customer experience.

"[Dealers] have been able to be laggards in this changing world, and we've required the customers to go through the drudgery. And so we [at Paragon] got excited and scared when we came to the realization that the second they can do business without us, they're going to."

The talk trigger at Paragon is the pickup and delivery of customers' vehicles. Of course, vehicle service and repair is the largest profit center for essentially every car dealer, so maximizing throughput in service is a huge priority. It's not terribly complex for most auto retailers. But if you're in New York City, there are inherent obstacles to being fast and convenient.

Benstock says Paragon was seeking a new location in Manhattan when it realized it would be a colossal hassle for many of their customers to get to whatever location they selected, given the typical gridlock on the island. Paragon's next idea was to build four drop-off points in north, south, east, and west Manhattan. But even that would be less than ideal for customers.

"So then we said, 'How about if we put a Honda dealership at every single address in Manhattan?'"

That was the inspiration for Paragon Direct: Benstock's team will pick up a customer's vehicle from any address in greater New York City; provide a loaner car if necessary; take the car to Paragon's location in Woodside, Queens; service it; and deliver it back to the customer's home or office address.

It's like Uber, except instead of requesting a car to appear, Paragon Direct customers request their car to be taken away and then returned—better than ever.

One of the challenges of implementing an all-virtual vehicle service program is how to explain to customers what needs to be done to their car or truck if they are not present at the dealership. So Paragon Direct created an enhanced method of customer communication and work approval.

Benstock says most service department experiences are less than optimal from a customer perspective. He sets the scene: "Bad coffee. Bad donuts. Jerry Springer or CNN on the television. Customer waited for an hour to get the car into the shop to have its tires rotated. And now you see the car needs new brakes. So the service advisor has to go get the customer and tell him or her that they need new brakes and rotors.

"And at that point, the customer has only two questions: 'How long?' and 'How much?' and will not like either answer."

But if the customer is at work or home, and his or her car is at Paragon, the customer is more likely to approve additional work, Benstock says. This is partially because of the transparency advantage of the web-based customer communication system. Paragon service advisors take a photo of the customer's brakes displayed alongside new brakes, to show the wear, and then asks the customer to approve the parts and labor. For more detailed work, the service advisors record a quick video explaining the proposed fix and why it's recommended.

"Being remote gives us more transparency and trust, not less. If you're sitting in the lobby of a dealership and you're told you need brakes, there's very little chance that you're going to be shown what your old brakes look like," Benstock explains.

In addition to the convenience of vehicle pickup and the increased trust from real-time work approvals with accompanying photos, Paragon Direct is also able to perform service faster than ever, even with delivery. How? Because it now keeps its service bays open twenty-four hours per day, seven days per week.

If customers don't need to be greeted, seen face-to-face, and plied with pastries, the service team can focus solely on service. And it gives customers even greater flexibility.

"We say to a customer, 'When do you stop using your car at night?' And if they say eight o'clock at night, then we will pick up the car at night, bring it to our service facility, service the car, and bring the car back to them before they need it the next morning," Benstock told us.

"It makes the best use of the ninety-four to ninety-six percent of the time when the car is not being driven. The customer wins, and we win."

Benstock says that the majority of dealers experience very little growth in service revenue, year over year. It's predominantly a profitable yet stagnant component of the business. Benstock's massively fast and super convenient pickup and drop-off system broke that trend line, yielding multiple record months in a row and overall growth of more than 20 percent since inception.

Picking up cars, servicing them overnight like a pack of wrench-wielding elves, and then returning them in the morning is a great example of talkable speed. Even more so because Paragon charges *nothing* for the Paragon Direct service.

Another way to create word of mouth with speed is to deliver to the customer not just immediately upon request, but even before the customer knows that she needs help.

KLM Royal Dutch Airlines

Based in Amsterdam, KLM is the official state airline of the Netherlands, and is one of the world's oldest commercial aviation companies, founded in 1919.

"People lose stuff on planes," says Karlijn Vogel-Meijer, global director of social media at KLM. "Usually, they put their iPads in a seat pocket or something like that. They forget about it, they run off the plane, and then, suddenly, their iPad is lost. What they usually do is they tweet or post and they say, 'OK, my iPad was in seat pocket 2D on this flight, going to this destination. Have you found it?'"

According to Vogel-Meijer, the airline's procedure used to be that fliers had to visit the company website and submit a lost items form. Then, after five days, customers could call KLM to see if the item had been found. It's a common albeit clunky process used by many airlines.

Most of the items lost on a plane, however, are quickly found by the flight attendants or cleaning crews as they prepare for the next flight. They used to take found items to the KLM transfer desk with a note that said "This was found in seat 2D," and hopefully the airline could match it up with the online forms a few days later. And Amsterdam is a major stopover on trans-Europe and other flight paths, which means many fliers who forget personal belongings on the plane are still in the airport waiting for their connecting flights when their items are found by the crew.

A member of Vogel-Meijer's social media team who works at the airport found a better way to reconnect customers with their lost items. Armed with only a tablet computer and a smartphone, this team member completely changed customer service from reactive to proactive. Without a committee meeting or official policy change—the KLM culture emphasizes employee initiatives—she asked flight crews to call her instead of taking found items to the KLM transfer desk. On her tablet she could then look up a customer's itinerary and discover that, say, his next flight was leaving from gate 37 to Paris in forty-five minutes.

"She rushes immediately to the gate, looks for Mr. Jensen, and tells him, 'Could it be that you lost something?' Mostly, they don't even know they have lost it yet, and suddenly they have their iPad back," explains Vogel-Meijer.

This proactive program has been so successful that it was expanded

Kostis A. Tselenis
@kotselen

Follow

@KLM great airline, excellent service and very responsive and professional in my case of a lost item in the plane! Keep on the good work!

7:09 AM - 12 Apr 2016

to an entire team at Schiphol airport, staffed mostly by flight crew members who are unable to fly due to pregnancy or other factors.

At present, this predictive approach is so unusual and unexpected that it creates customer chatter. After all, if you were at an airport gate waiting to board a flight and a uniformed airline crew member sauntered up alongside and delivered your iPad, it would seem like sorcery.

This talk trigger is powerful for KLM right now, but it may not last forever. Customer expectations change, especially in the area of speed and responsiveness. In fact, according to research from Walker, "The customer of 2020 . . . will expect companies to know their individual needs and personalize the experience. Immediate resolution will not be fast enough as customers will expect companies to proactively address their current and future needs."

We'll investigate the life cycle of talk triggers in chapter 19. But first, let's look at the fifth and final way to clone customers with word of mouth: talkable attitude.

CHAPTER 12

Talkable Attitude

When asked to describe businesses as a whole, customers may consider several adjectives. Some of them may involve four letters, but very rarely would one of them be "dope."

Indeed, while you might expect a heavy dose of ennui from your undertaker and a taciturn timbre from your accountant, it seems like just about all businesses are pretty darn serious, or at least inoffensively vanilla, in their tone.

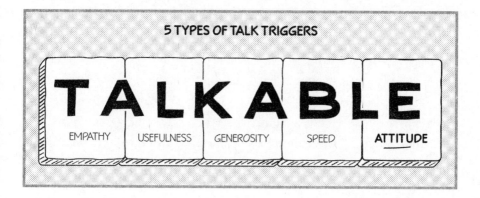

5 TYPES OF TALK TRIGGERS

TALKABLE

EMPATHY   USEFULNESS   GENEROSITY   SPEED   ATTITUDE

This presents a huge opportunity to defy customer expectations with joie de vivre and flair, creating a talk trigger from attitude.

Jay Baer's tailor is the master of this approach. Kaleb Ryan is the proprietor of Elevated Citizen, showcasing his EC Chantal clothing line. Ryan is a custom menswear clothier who visits his clients in their homes and offices throughout the United States and then designs high-quality suits and outerwear at reasonable prices.

In addition to being a master craftsman with an extraordinary attention to detail—Kaleb Ryan offers hundreds of different kinds of buttons alone—he also refuses to adhere to the stuffy standards typically associated with menswear.

This attitude is perhaps best expressed by Ryan's commitment to hidden messages embedded in his work. Every EC Chantal suit has three canvases for Ryan's wordplay: inside the jacket, on the breast pocket; underneath the jacket collar; and on the fly of the pants, when unzipped.

Ryan has always added these humorous and ironic touches, although his ability to be creative was initially curbed by tailoring limitations. "At first, the customization code [a technique used to define and manufacture the garment] would only allow for two letters, so it was initials only," says Ryan.

Now, with nineteen characters to play with, Ryan goes wild, and nearly every client not only talks about these messages but also gives him free reign to write them. It is a special kind of anticipation when you get a new custom suit and you immediately grab the pants zipper to see what Ryan has written there. Unzip Jay's new suit, and it reads, TALK TRIGGERS.

Ryan also makes shirts and is considering launching a denim line. But as a suit specialist, it's unlikely he'll ever offer terry cloth headbands as an EC Chantal item. Fortunately, Uberflip—another example of talkable attitude—can step into that breach.

Uberflip

Founded by Yoav Schwartz and Randy Frisch in Toronto, Ontario, in 2012, Uberflip is a B2B software company that empowers marketers to create remarkable content experiences using their video, white papers, blog posts, and social media.

Uberflip's software makes it easier for digital marketers to do their job—and easier for potential customers to interact with content created by those marketers. "When we realized the company was going to center on making things easy, we also realized we couldn't take ourselves too seriously," Frisch told us in an interview.

One of the ways the company adheres to this premise is through unbridled use of pink as its signature shade. Everything at Uberflip is pink: a color not typically associated with B2B software.

"We didn't want to go with 1980s neon pink, and we definitely didn't want baby pink. It took us a long time to select," says Frisch. "The actual color is called rubine red. It's technically a shade of red, but to everyone who sees it, it's pink." (It's the color on the cover of this book.)

The second way Uberflip departs from the norm is by pulling back the curtain on the marketing and sales process. This is especially effective because Uberflip is selling to marketers who are, as a rule, as jaded as an aging New Kids fan still bitter about the breakup.

"At first, we used the typical generic-drip emails like: 'Hi, I'm Steve and I'm from the Uberflip team. Contact me and I'll help you,'" says Frisch. "I looked around and said: 'We're bullshitting these people. They know these emails are automated. They know exactly what we're doing.'"

Frisch and his team replaced the drippy, fake Steve with an even more artificial personage: Katie. But this time, they let the potential customer in on the routine. The first email read "Hi, I'm Katie. I'm going to level with you since you're a B2B marketer as well. I'm not real, but a lot of thought was put into who I'm going to be by our marketing team. So, please enjoy the upcoming emails because our marketing team really thinks about every word that I'm going to tell you. We're going to level with you and treat you with respect. You're knowledgeable, so we're going to throw everything out on the table. Here's why we think we can help you do your job better. Let us know if you want to talk."

The pink is different. So is the candor. But the real talk trigger for Uberflip is even further afield, rivaled in the pantheon of this book only by WindsorONE's Call Kurt for a Shirt word-of-mouth engine. For Uberflip, it's all about the headbands.

In the early days of the company, Frisch handled all marketing and promotions. Uberflip was cosponsoring a bash at the influential South by Southwest (SXSW) technology event in Austin, Texas, and needed some sort of giveaway for partygoers.

Frisch remembers exactly what happened next. "I went to Google and I searched 'rubine red swag,' and on the first page, I found these headbands that had a minimum order of only one hundred and cost less than three dollars each. It was literally a seven-minute investigation."

One of the not-so-secret secrets of SXSW is that conference attendees RSVP to every conceivable party and then show up to only a handful. The Uberflip affair was no different, with three thousand RSVPs to a party where ninety people walked through the door to claim a headband.

Frisch and his small team went back to Toronto with ten remaining headbands and an email list of three thousand people who presumably knew nearly nothing about the company. The usual approach is to email the entire list with a "sorry you couldn't make it, but here's what our software does" message.

That's the zig. Frisch zagged.

The headline of Uberflip's post-SXSW follow-up email was, "You forgot your headband at the party." It contained a photo of Frisch and three customers, wearing the shockingly pink headbands, and a simple message: "If you want your headband, we've only got ten. Let us know if you want one, and we'll send it to you."

In seventy-five minutes, one hundred fifty people requested headbands. "We didn't hesitate to order more; after all, people wanted to wear our brand on their head!" explained Frisch.

Spotting a trend, Uberflip began to use the headbands everywhere in its marketing, encouraging people to snap photos of how they're using their headbands.

Uberflip has distributed more than twenty thousand since, and the pink headband has become a talk trigger.

"People come up to us at conferences all the time and say, 'You guys are the headband company. I've got mine on my desk at the office,'" Frisch says.

UberConference

It's not strictly required that a business looking to utilize attitude as a talk trigger also include the word *uber* in the company name, but evidently it doesn't hurt, given that our third example of word of mouth through tone and tenor comes from UberConference.

In the previous chapter, we mentioned that more than nine in ten American consumers refuse to wait on hold for longer than five minutes. Maybe that's because so many businesses are equal parts awkward and pushy when designing their on-hold music and messages.

There seems to be two schools of thought with regard to what to present to a customer while she is on hold. The first is the "tranquility approach," wherein the company attempts to calm a customer's potential ire with ultrasoothing tunes, typically featuring lots and lots of saxophone. The second is the "we hired Jimmy Buffett to play our son's bris" angle, when the company seizes upon the captive nature of the audience and decides it's a fantastic time to try to sell more stuff.

UberConference opts for door number three, using hold time as a chance to add a little lightness and levity into the day of callers, few of whom are dialing in thinking, "Yay! A conference call!"

Founded in San Francisco in 2012, UberConference is a web-based audio conference call platform that also includes the ability to share documents on-screen. UberConference is free for calls with ten participants or fewer. This is, of course, a great price. As a result, UberConference is very popular with small businesses, and many thousands of calls are placed on the system every hour.

Most participants who log in to UberConference before the "host" of the call has joined will hear the now famous on-hold song, which has become the brand's talk trigger. One of the features of UberConference is the ability to upload custom on-hold music, but the default song is so good that few customers take the time to change it.

Like Uberflip's email from "Katie" that acknowledged she was an invention of the marketing team, the UberConference folk and country–inspired song embraces the boredom and inanity of waiting on hold instead of trying to pretend it is either stimulating or useful. Some of the lyrics are as follows:

> Well I been sittin' here all day I been sitting in this waiting room
> And I been I waiting on my friends, yes I'm
> Waiting on this conference call, all alone
> And I'm on hold
> Yes, I'm on hold
> I hope it's not all day
> haha

The song was written by the cofounder and creative director of UberConference, Alex Cornell, who told *Fast Company* magazine, "It really surprises people in a fun way; we get a lot of tweets about it, every day, which is cool."

The song certainly does create a lot of customer chatter, and

CEO Craig Walker says the song is one of the most-discussed Uber-
Conference features.

Olivier Travers
@otravers

Follow

Just got to an @uberconference 1 hour too
early, which was totally worth it thanks to
their awesome on hold country music

11:06 AM - 22 Nov 2017

Christine Bader
@christinebader

Follow

I stumbled on @uberconference looking for a
new free conference call service; I found the
service good, but I just heard the hold music
and they've now got me for life.

"I'm On Hold" with Scott Bradlee & Postmodern Jukebox - ...
YouTube sensation Scott Bradlee & Postmodern Jukebox have
tackled a new challenge – bringing Alex Cornell's hit "I'm On
Hold" to our users in a new way. In September 2012, one of our
blog.uberconference.com

8:20 AM - 18 Dec 2017

Hamed Abbasi
@iamhamedabbasi

Follow

The hold music on @uberconference calls is
the coolest thing I've witnessed in years.

11:11 AM - 5 Sep 2017 from Toronto, Ontario

1 Like

Go ahead and set up your own UberConference and listen in for yourself. Or go to TalkTriggers.com and you'll find a link to both the standard version, performed by Cornell, and the newfangled version created by YouTube sensations and touring musical artists Scott Bradlee and the Postmodern Jukebox. *(Warning: You will NOT be able to get either version of the song out of your head for a while. Do not listen unless you are going to set this book aside until tomorrow!)*

Talkable attitude can be a very effective word-of-mouth propagator, but it has to fit the cultural DNA of the company to be authentic and believable. Note that at Uberflip, the pink headbands came from cofounder Randy Frisch. At UberConference, the on-hold song was written and recorded by cofounder Alex Cornell. This is not a coincidence.

It's not a requirement that founders or executives craft your talk trigger. In fact, most of the examples in this book were not developed by senior leaders. If you're going to pursue attitude as your talk trigger archetype, however, it needs to be embraced at every level of the organization, including the highest reaches. Attitude has to "feel" true to work as a talk trigger, and that can happen only if everyone is on board.

Speaking of getting others on board with your talk trigger, that's what we'll cover in the final section of the book. In chapters 13 through 19, we'll show you precisely how to find, develop, launch, and measure your own talk triggers.

You know the four requirements that need to be present for a differentiator to be a talk trigger. And now that this chapter has concluded, you know the five types of talk triggers. Are you ready to learn how to make your own?

Before we show you the six-step process for talk trigger construction, rollout, and measurement, how's it going for you at this point? What's your feedback on the book? What questions can we answer for you? Take a minute to send us a note at JayAndDaniel@Talk Triggers.com, and we'll reply right away.

SECTION 4

Create Talk Triggers in Six Steps

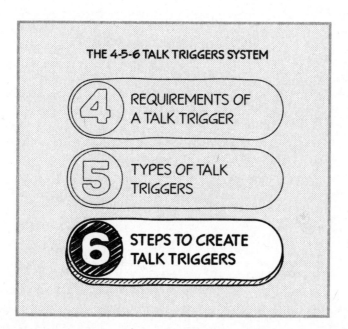

THE 4-5-6 TALK TRIGGERS SYSTEM

4 REQUIREMENTS OF A TALK TRIGGER

5 TYPES OF TALK TRIGGERS

6 STEPS TO CREATE TALK TRIGGERS

Y ou've learned about the four requirements that set talk triggers apart from stunts and gimmicks, and now you've identified the five types of talk triggers. We could leave you here, armed with the basics of talk trigger architecture, and hope that you end up with something usable.

But we realized that simply illuminating and classifying talk triggers is a bit like handing a copy of *Architectural Digest* to someone standing in the plumbing aisle at The Home Depot. You're here to build something, not just look at what others have done. You have to see the mess while it's in progress to better understand how these ideas go from concept to customer conversation. Understanding how talk triggers are built and managed will help you create something truly unique, remarkable, and durable for your own organization.

So in this section we're going to look at how you systematically go about the six steps for researching, testing, and deploying talk triggers, which is the 6 in the 4-5-6 system.

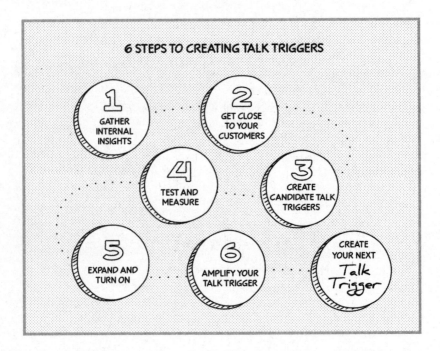

Most of us will be lucky to be given the chance to build a talk trigger even once in our careers. It's not that talk triggers are that rare; indeed, as we've discovered through the case studies in this book, they're quite common. But talk triggers are unique because they're not generally owned by any one function in a company. The marketing department might manage them in one instance, whereas the founders of a company built them in another (as was the case at

Lockbusters, Uberflip, UberConference, and at many of our other case studies).

When we were doing interviews for this book, we spent a good deal of time with each company to better understand the process that led to its talk trigger. How did they come up with the idea, overcome inertia to make it happen, and identify the right metrics to guide the decision(s) to keep it going?

What we discovered was an interesting pattern. Despite the variety of original champions for talk trigger ideas, the actual process of adoption is very similar in most organizations: It reflects a commitment to customers. Companies in this book did interviews. They tested ideas, looking for moments when they could make a customer smile. They looked for ideas that could become storytelling fodder. And in almost every case, they were fanatical about listening to customers.

We gathered what we learned into this six-step process for identifying, testing, and managing talk triggers. The process works because it's focused on doing something different. The steps here are sequential and systematic, though how they manifest in different organizations may vary. Smaller organizations may find some steps go faster than they do for larger ones, whereas larger organizations may find some economies of scale with other research efforts they already direct toward customer listening.

Following these six steps will help you to accomplish the results you seek—building strategic, repeatable, and meaningful differentiators for your business that keep customers talking about you.

Slay Obstacle Dragons

Another bit of insight we discovered in our interviews: To be effective with initiatives like talk triggers requires both great process *and* great mind-set. It is exceptionally rare for a great idea to be born and immediately thrive. Talk triggers behave a lot like products: They need constant evolution, optimization, refinement, and user feedback. Decent talk triggers can become outstanding talk triggers with minor changes. And, naturally, outstanding talk triggers can become irrelevant when market dynamics change. You need to be in the right mind-set to avoid frustration and help sustain momentum.

Managing internal obstacles and being the champion of the process is your particular burden to bear as a talk trigger leader in your organization. We found that the spirit of the "obstacle slayer" is a very meaningful mind-set to embrace straight out of the gate. You'll encounter naysayers right away, and you might become frustrated when ideas don't seem to stick the first time around. It's important for that reason that you don't get too attached to any one idea or concept.

As Godin wrote in *Purple Cow*, "You do not equal the project. Criticism of the project is *not* criticism of you."

Before you get rolling into the six-step process, would it be helpful for you to connect with peers in other organizations who are going through many of these same challenges? As a reader of *Talk Triggers* you are also a member of the exclusive Talk Triggers community. It's an online group of word-of-mouth fans and compatriots. Go to TalkTriggers.com and learn how to log on at no cost. We'll be there to welcome you and help you celebrate every single step you're about to take!

CHAPTER 13

Gather Internal Insights

Your head may be swimming with ideas at this point. Perhaps one of those ideas is the perfect one! But do your ideas pass the test of the four criteria for a talk trigger? Are you wondering which of the five types of talk triggers might work best for you and your business?

Terrific!

Now let's put those ideas into action to leave a trail of logic that others in your organization can understand so that when you find the right idea, and it sticks, you can stick with it and keep the talk trigger going. Begin by gathering the internal insights that will help you to understand the type of talk trigger that is right for your organization and by addressing several other possible challenges that you may face later on in the process.

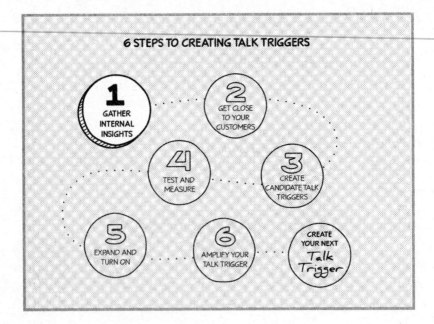

Who Knows What?

The first step toward creating effective word of mouth in your organization is to unlock everything already known about your customers—what they want and how they use the products and services offered by your business. It's internal anthropology.

But one of the challenges of talk trigger creation—and in maintaining word-of-mouth programs through the years—is that it's not really "owned" by a particular department. In reality, everybody owns word of mouth, because it takes all corners of the organization (whether the business is small or large) to deliver on the differentiator every time.

Word of mouth often doesn't fit nicely into your organization chart. Is it the owner's responsibility? Or does it belong to marketing? Operations? Sales? Customer service? The answer is yes. All the above have to be involved, and more.

There is no talk trigger without a great idea. But where do great ideas come from? Where is their nesting ground? Do they hide under bridges, like trolls? It's possible that your great idea will magically appear during a sales call, in a customer support conversation, or even while listening to a Keith Urban record in the lunchroom.

But "waiting for inspiration" is an unreliable method for creating a talk trigger. Or for creating much of anything, really. What you need instead is an actual system and a team of skilled people who can delve into data, interpret it, and then draw outside the lines—a team committed to making word of mouth work.

In any organization there are likely to be people with strong opinions about what the talk triggers should be. When strategizing about who should be involved in a talk trigger effort, think beyond job function and title. Who are your company's most vocal employee advocates? Who was hired because they're already a power user, or because they launched a fan club?

In his book *Fizz*, Ted Wright reminds us why employees are so important to our goal of boosting conversation: "Never forget that your employees are talking about your company no matter what. They are members of the community too. Whether you like it or not, they are acting as brand ambassadors when they leave at the end of the day."

Create Your Talk Triggers Triangle of Awesome

The people you include in a talk triggers team can, to some degree, determine the outcome of the effort. Leave it to the marketing team and you're likely to end up with another collection of campaign ideas. Although that's not unhelpful, remind yourself what a talk trigger is: a strategic, operational differentiator that makes word of mouth involuntary.

Talk triggers aren't gimmicks; they're business choices.

A new product flavor is not a talk trigger. New eco-friendly packaging is (most likely) not a talk trigger. Those are, at best, undifferentiated and gimmicky at worst.

Assembling the right team is one way you defend against gimmickry. In her book *More Is More*, author Blake Morgan reminds us of the inherent institutional knowledge held by employees.

"Employees have extremely detailed knowledge about what creates value for customers and what works for the business. Involving customer-facing staff in creative design helps decrease your chances of failure. The significant by-product is highly engaged staff that will embrace the improvement and change they were part of creating."

So who do you call on to be part of a talk triggers creation team? We call it the Triangle of Awesome.

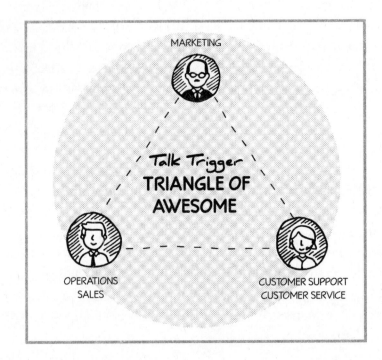

The Triangle of Awesome includes one or more representatives from marketing, sales, and customer service. If you have market research personnel in your business, they should absolutely be part of your team, too, as should outside advertising or marketing agencies with whom you may interact, especially if they have good knowledge of your customers.

You are including marketing for obvious reasons; they'll be the ones who are tasked with fostering conversation about the talk trigger among fans, customers, employees, and other stakeholders. But the main reason to have marketing on the team is its position in the organization's heart.

Marketing is often considered the most exciting part of business. It's all about real people and the connection we build with them over time as a brand. Done efficiently, great marketing is about capturing and cultivating momentum. These are the roots of a great talk trigger culture.

Likewise, your sales and/or operations teams will be fearless advocates for solving customer problems. They're witnessing daily the struggles customers are having and what's missing in the marketplace. The insights from the sales team can unlock paths of exploration for talk trigger ideas, concepts that may be too esoteric for actual product design but might resonate as a talk trigger.

Your customer service team is your secret talk trigger weapon, as it's the closest to day-to-day issues. The team knows what worries concern your customers. It is the first line of defense for problem solving, and focusing on customer dissatisfaction is one of the best methods for uncovering talk triggers that will be meaningful to those same customers long term.

We call this approach a Triangle of Awesome because it involves three perspectives on your customer: your market position (marketing), your unique selling proposition (operations and sales), and day-to-day customer interaction (service). We've heard many times during our work as consultants that companies routinely struggle to foster collaboration among these groups, even knowing how important it is. You may find that the assembling of a talk trigger team in and of itself can be an enlightening and constructive exercise.

We'll give you specific exercises and tasks for this team in the chapters to come, but you can start by setting ground rules from the beginning. These will make the talk triggers team a space for broad thinking and iteration. And you should give each member of your new team some assignments to bring to a first meeting.

Talk Triggers Team Assignments

For the marketing team, ask it to assemble the following data points for both your company and some competitors.

BRAND POSITIONING

Most companies, even small ones, have documented their brand voice and personality. This organizational gestalt can help reframe and refocus conversation later on in the process, so it's helpful to revisit it now.

CURRENT WORD-OF-MOUTH AND SOCIAL MEDIA TRENDS

Ask the marketing minds to bring some current research and thinking about word-of-mouth trends, either from within your own organization's research archive or from general industry publications. Anecdotal evidence here is enough to get you started and contributing to the conversation. We'll look at social media data again in more detail in the next chapter. For now, stick to the trend lines.

COMPETITIVE POSITIONING

How does your brand stack up against competitors, and what sets you apart? Although talk triggers do not necessarily need to draw directly from this competitive position—plenty of them do not—it can help at least to generate initial ideas.

MARKET RESEARCH

We've purposefully left this a broad category, but it will be meaningful for your team to look at current consumer behavior data along with economic and spending forecasts. What are the analyst predictions for trends that will shape your industry? Sometimes a talk trigger is connected directly to one of these trends. That was the case for Air New Zealand, which chose to redouble its efforts to improve the economy class cabin in which most of its customers travel.

CUSTOMER RETENTION SURVEYS

You can assess customer retention from a couple of different approaches. The question you want to ask here is: Why do customers continue to do business with us today?

NET PROMOTER SCORE ANALYSIS

Some organizations are borderline fanatical about their Net Promoter Score (NPS), and we're big fans of it ourselves. Viewed over time, NPS can give a peek at organizational performance and customer loyalty. If you track NPS, ask how the health of your organization's score is. Does it head up and to the right, or has it reached a plateau? This and your customer retention insights could help unlock an opportunity for a talk trigger.

You probably don't need to commission a whole new primary research study to help you identify talk triggers. Indeed, that can send you down multiple distracting rabbit holes. Customers are not great at telling you proactively what they really need.

Author Youngme Moon describes this problem succinctly: "Here is the problem with formal market research. Consumers will always be able to tell us how much better they'd like our products to be. But we cannot expect them to be able to tell us how different those products *could be*. And more important, we cannot expect them to tell us how it might be possible for us to surprise them."

That makes sense when you think about it: If you're about to get engaged and want to truly surprise your spouse with something he or she will talk about forever, are you just going to ask about his or her dream engagement setting? Such lack of imagination may not sit well with your future spouse.

Your operations and sales teams have access to different types of customer data and insights than your marketing team, so their assignment list looks different:

WIN/LOSS DATA

When your sales team is in a competitive pitch, it's vital to understand why you're winning or losing. What makes a customer choose you or, alternatively, choose a competitor? What are the specific value propositions that your competitors are using to win over customers who are otherwise sitting on the fence? How are competitors describing their product and the promise it holds?

PRODUCT REQUESTS

Among current and renewing customers, or those loyal to your company, what are the most requested product features or additions that you haven't yet introduced?

CUSTOMER ANECDOTES AND MEGAFANS

What does the operations team hear from the field about what is on customers' minds? What does product usage tell us about how customers are responding to or interacting with the product? You want to examine some insights from your megafans and power users. Why do they love your company so much? What about your product makes them such huge fans?

CUSTOMER CHURN DATA

We referenced earlier in the chapter one way of viewing customer retention. There's a different way of framing the same question: Why did people stop doing business with you?

This data will give you some perspective on where you are currently winning in the market and may help you to better frame elements of your talk triggers approach.

The beauty of working in customer service or customer support is that these team members are consistently exposed to both the real-world problems customers are facing and the underlying customer psychology behind those issues. These support professionals are your organizational mood rings. Ask them to bring their reading of the tea leaves.

CALL CENTER LOGS

In larger organizations you'll often find a long list of gems hidden in call center logs. Those are the massive spreadsheets that detail customer interactions—what they're calling about, where they're calling from, what customer segment they fit into, and so on. This data paints a very detailed picture of your customers' behaviors, needs, and desires.

ANECDOTES

Your customer support personnel have daily contact with customers, just like your operations and sales teams. The tone and tenor of customer support conversations will obviously be markedly different, however, so ask this team to bring its own anecdotes about customer behaviors, mind-set, and wants and needs.

You may also find value in conducting an internal survey of your customer-facing teams to help you discover things that might not get said in a boardroom or reported on a call center log. Are there specific problems your client service team wishes it could solve? Is there a common request that it doesn't have the tools to fulfill?

Think about KLM, which launched a talk trigger by massively overhauling how it handled lost items at the airport. This initiative was not mandated by the executive team; it was devised by a single employee in a customer service role who understood that a better way to handle lost items was possible.

At FreshBooks, cofounder Mike McDerment describes how his client services team is systematically empowered to deliver small storytelling moments for customers.

"We were following one of our customers on Twitter and we saw that she got stood up for a date. We sent her a bouquet of flowers saying, 'Hey, we'd never stand you up.' You sort of can't plan these things. You gotta be open and then sort of, you know, take action."

At that level of execution, what the FreshBooks team is accomplishing is not quite an actual talk trigger. It actually borders on being a surprise-and-delight stunt, which is not a talk trigger. But the idea behind it has the potential to be operationalized further and turned into a real differentiator that capitalizes on our key requirements and sets FreshBooks apart from other accounting software providers. What other software company on the planet have you heard about that sends its customers flowers? These are the elements that a client services team can bring to the table that can open doors to talk triggers.

Ground Rules for Insights Gathering

An initial talk triggers meeting is nothing more than a report of the assignments listed above. You shouldn't create ideas or discuss possibilities or their viability. That's a tough mind-set, because we all want to solve problems once we've identified what they are. But you cannot do that successfully until you've heard all the data and given space for some broader thinking. Each member (or group, if there are multiple attendees from each) should give a report about the current state of affairs.

You'll also need to nominate a worthy scribe to take notes during the meeting. What you're looking for are bullet points:

- X percent of our customers don't have cars.
- X percent of our customers complain about ice cream being too frozen.
- We hear from customers that they'd like more colors.
- People say our packaging is hard to open.

- We lose customers to Brand B because they love the mascot logo.
- Our power users think we save their jobs by preventing bad decisions.

You'll end up with a list of these—a simple document that should be shared with the team as the beginning of your internal insights. That's really the end of your first meeting. Nothing more complicated is needed. But you cannot create talk triggers in one meeting, and in our experience, gathering and analyzing insights and dreaming up ideas use different parts of the brain, so we'll treat them differently.

The next step in the talk triggers process will be to gather additional customer data and craft personas to help you understand more about customers' quirks, their needs, and their personalities. The initial report from the assignments above will help you explore what those next questions need to be. In the next chapter we'll look at where you find that data, how you access it, and what you do with it.

And remember that we have loads of other resources for you, including how-to guides, charts, presentation templates, and a lot more. It's all waiting at TalkTriggers.com.

CHAPTER 14

Get Close to Your Customers

She passed away."

Daniel Lemin worked in the communications department at a credit card company early in his career. Part of his role was to sit in on calls at the call center and listen to customer conversations. This was a ritual everyone in the company was encouraged to take part in to help build empathy for the customers and their interactions with the product.

During one very memorable call, a customer asked to close an account. Such calls generally follow a routine script—literally. This particular situation was more difficult, however, because the customer was unable to provide the verification needed to access the account. Typically, calls to a credit card lender are made by the cardholder. In this instance, the caller's sister had passed away suddenly. Her family was attempting to resolve outstanding financial obligations as part of her estate.

It took the customer service rep by surprise when the customer's sister finally admitted that she was not the cardholder, but in fact the cardholder had passed away.

Flummoxed that the caller did not know the security word, the representative fumbled to find the right internal process to address the situation. Eventually, she found the right part of her script and was able to help the customer solve the problem. It created an awkward pause on the call, a gap that neither the customer nor the customer service representative could quite fill. It was a memorable call for Daniel because it illustrated one vitally important point: You cannot possibly know how your customer will interact with your product. Even if you write 993 call scripts, you'll encounter a 994th scenario quickly.

It is impossible to know everything about a customer from market research, annual surveys, and call center logs. So, unsurprisingly, it can be difficult to create talk trigger ideas that will surprise a customer enough to share the story with their friends and family from the comfort of a conference room. What doesn't surface in most surveys are the things a customer actually needs. Sure, they can rank what they *want* on a scale from 1 to 10—more speed, lower prices, faster processors, or more sandwich topping variety— but rarely do they tell you what they really need.

Think back to Dr. Glenn Gorab in chapter 8: The singular insight that it would be, perhaps, a good idea to call patients *before* their surgery rather than after, as most other surgeons do, was framed by customer empathy—an understanding that patients may feel more at ease hearing from a doctor ahead of dental surgery. A survey might have suggested what customers wanted: a call from the doctor. What would have been missing is the subtlety of when the call happens: before, to help a patient manage their nerves and insurance anxiety, rather than after.

Surveys and research tell you primarily about what customers say they want at a surface level. That's valuable stuff and can certainly be the source of a talk trigger. But rarely can a consumer, in a survey environment, actually share what they *really* need and what will exceed expectations. You might learn in a survey that they want a lower priced product. Does that mean slashing prices will help generate word of mouth for your brand? Probably not. You've simply met expectations.

The same distinction can be seen with Penn & Teller's ritual of greeting guests after their shows. They do it because, after such a memorable performance, people don't want the magic to end. They don't need a meet and greet with Penn & Teller. What they *really* want is for the moment to last. That's why their approach works so well and generates so much word of mouth. Copperfield's approach—charging extra for a meet and greet experience and available only on certain nights—doesn't create word of mouth because it's just as expected.

That shadowy space between what a customer wants and what a customer *really* wants is the exact space where talk triggers often live.

To help illuminate the darkness in that gap, it's necessary to get as close as possible to the customer.

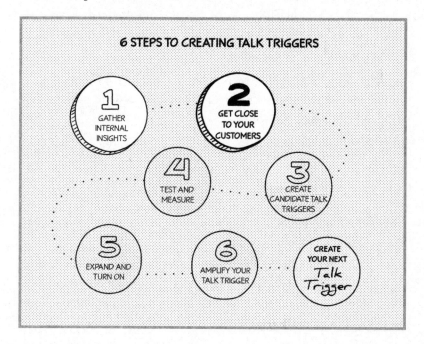

Getting Your Team Close to Your Customers

Your talk triggers team—that Triangle of Awesome from chapter 13—all have very different data and different perspectives on the customer. As outlined in the last chapter, your first talk triggers meeting will be a reading of currently known data from each of the team members' domains.

From that initial meeting you'll begin to collectively ask other questions. Most likely you won't have any data that answers them. They can be hard questions, such as the following:

- How do our customers experience our product?
- Why do our customers refer us today?
- What do our customers say about our brand, unaided?
- What do our customers say about our competitors or partners, unaided?
- Where in the product experience is the right time for us to introduce a talk trigger?

Hard questions like those can be answered only by getting as close as possible to your customers. You have a variety of mechanisms for accomplishing that objective, so let's review them one by one.

Customer Surveys

Survey data isn't usually the source of inspiration, and that's OK. You should use the data from your current customer insights efforts to begin framing what you currently know, which you probably did in the last step (detailed in chapter 13). This gives you an initial perspective on customer behavior, opinions, and possibly even psychographics.

It is especially helpful to use survey data as a benchmark for customer experience expectations over time. What customers might have valued in your product even nine months ago may have changed. For instance, when was the last time you used the cigarette lighter in your car, if it even has one? And yet, in many vehicles, power adapters (USB or a plug) are still optional. The need for power has become universal for most consumers, while many have stopped smoking. Addressing these small shifts and changes won't necessarily win you any awards, but you may avoid something very detrimental to the future success of your talk triggers: word-of-mouth enemies.

Taking the power outlet example above, it's entirely possible to create a vehicle cabin worthy of Instagram, but small things—like lack of power outlets—may hold you back from fulfilling your destiny. It becomes just as worthy of mention in a consumer's eyes as your actual talk trigger. "It's great that the car has a diamond-encrusted steering wheel, but there's no way to charge my phone. Fail."

Getting those small things right puts you on par with your competitors and slays these enemies of word of mouth.

Social Media Conversation Data

It was encouraging to us when we did the research for this book just how much word of mouth still happens offline. Our analysis, and many other research projects, reinforces the value of offline word of mouth. Does social media still matter?

Yes.

In fact, approximately 50 percent of all word of mouth is online, according to Engagement Labs research.

Could you have a BLT without bacon, or a jazz trio without a pianist? Possibly, but the vast majority of the best BLTs benefit from bacon, and most jazz trios have a pianist. Social media is a component of word of mouth, one that both helps establish the pass-along value of a talk trigger and also reflects how your customers perceive your brand.

There are some considerations when looking at social media data. For example, the tone and tenor of social media conversation about your brand may skew toward extremes that do not reflect the majority of your customers. The type of conversation about a brand on social media can reflect the interests of only a small percentage of your customer population, inaccurately skewing your initial analysis.

As we covered in chapter 2, our research with Audience Audit reinforced how wide the gap can be between offline and online word of mouth: More than nine in ten respondents had mentioned DoubleTree or The Cheesecake Factory face-to-face, whereas fewer than three in ten had done so on social media.

It could safely be presumed, then, that social media assists conversion of a talk trigger into actual word-of-mouth conversation. Unlike some other concepts that you might have tested in the past, social media conversation is not the primary goal of a talk trigger; rather, it is a by-product. This is what separates a talk trigger from, say, a "surprise and delight" strategy aimed at top influencers and unavailable to your full customer community.

What do you look for in social data, then? It's less about you and more about your customer. Social data helps you quantify what's popular, how willing your customers are to share information about the brands in their lives, and what's influencing them. It is somewhat easy, using almost any available social media monitoring tool, to access word clouds and content insights.

Twitter, since its earliest days, has had a surprisingly simple prompt: What's happening?

Let that be the question you ask when parsing your social data: What's happening with my customers? Looking at your social data over a range of time will help you normalize the data for externalities that caused a spike in either positive or negative discussion.

While you're at it, run the same set of reports you create for your own brand for your competitors. Even better is to run it for the brands that you admire, especially those from other sectors.

Product or Service Usage Data

We wrote earlier that you cannot always predict how customers will use your product. If you build something with one set of features in mind, you may find that the ingenuity of your customer base outsmarts you and finds a different—perhaps more novel—way to experience it.

No better example of this exists than the now not-so-secret secret menu at In-N-Out Burger. The fast-food chain famously has a limited menu, the staple being hamburgers available with or without cheese. For some guests that's not a very exciting menu. But the restaurant enjoys an almost rabid fan base.

With little fanfare and almost no traditional marketing support, the company embraces its customers' desire to customize the menu. You can order multiple patties and multiple slices of cheese, grilled onions instead of fresh, or a lettuce wrap instead of a bun. The permutations are not endless, but they create enough variety and intrigue that it keeps the ritual going. And it's not how the company even intends for its core product to be consumed. Today, the menu continues to list four basic options: a hamburger (single or double) and a cheeseburger (single or double).

Sales Conversations, Interviews, and Customer Service Calls

Be honest: When was the last time you actually heard the voice of a real customer?

It can seem almost wasteful to spend valuable time sitting with just one customer, but what you learn from that experience can transform how you think about your own company and brand. In many start-up programs—including the well-regarded technology incubator Y Combinator—it is an actual objective for the company's founders to talk to at least a handful of real, live customers every single week.

The good news is that a well-structured talk triggers team can bring some scale to those conversations. If you've got your sales colleagues on the team—and you should, if you've embraced the Triangle of Awesome—you'll have their daily experience talking with prospective customers to guide you. Ditto for the customer service team, which can share its insights with you from the other end of the customer journey.

You'll find it valuable to get on the phone (or in-person) with at least a handful of customers and ask them to share their experiences with you. Begin with that list of questions you formed during the initial talk triggers meeting. You're not looking for quantitative findings here. You're really looking to hear about the customer's experience and perspective, why he or she loves (or does not love) your product, and what the customer loves about the other brands he or she is loyal to.

When we launch a consulting project, during the kickoff discovery call we always end with an important question: What will make you feel that this project has been successful?

It's always nice to end with a final open-ended question of this nature when you're talking with customers: How do we, as a brand, make you feel today?

If the customer's reply is "not much," you'll see clearly how much work you have ahead of you. Nobody talks about products or experiences that don't leave them feeling something. This is the thing that separates an undifferentiated product benefit from a talk trigger, and it's a concept that you need to view through a different lens. Sometimes when customers don't have strong feelings about a brand, we need to revisit just why things might be leaving them quiet.

Living the Customer Experience

Here's another question, and be honest again: When was the last time you experienced your own product or that of your competitors?

All the research, social data, and demographics in the world cannot replace on-the-ground experience. Going even part of the way through the sales process or product experience on your own can sharpen your awareness of gaps where the experience lags, when examining for things like how a competitor positions its product or what content it creates around it.

In his book *What Customers Crave*, Nicholas Webb describes this as contact point innovation, or "inventing at the point at which the experience is being delivered rather than in the boardroom or laboratory, far away from where customers actually experience the service or product."

If yours is a product that can be purchased in a retail environment, you might find it fun to bring a child along for the experience. A young mind sees the world free from prejudice of price, promotion, or place. You might catch an idea simply by watching how his or her young mind contemplates one product over another.

Another way to experience your product is to examine the experience in the margins. If you have an invoice-based business, have you ever let your account go to collections?

Tom Karinshak, executive VP of customer service at the large television, internet, phone, and home security company Comcast, does this regularly. Why? He wants to see the entirety of the customer experience, at both its best and worst points. An amazing product with a nasty surprise in the collections department will lead to an undesirable product for at least some percentage of your customer base. It's a talk trigger, to be sure, but of the wrong kind.

As you saw in chapter 8, the team at Americollect knows that and created an entire business because of it. You know what else is fascinating about Americollect's business? More than 60 percent of its call center team were at one time Americollect customers. They owed medical bills and, based on their excellent experience with the company, chose to apply for a job.

Create Personas

As you go through these exercises and experiences, you will naturally begin answering some of those questions from your first talk triggers meeting. You'll begin to understand your customers better. How you frame your thinking about customers and customer behavior bears remarkable similarity to another technique you might be familiar with: customer personas. Generally, a customer persona is a fictional character that represents your ideal or typical customer. Sometimes they're even snapshots of a real customer who represents the average or ideal one.

These are powerful because they're relatable. And they work only when they're documented and written down, so do yourself a favor here: Document your insights! We've developed some templates at TalkTriggers.com for you to do just that. Download and use them, or riff off them and create something of your own design. Documenting the knowledge you've gathered will not only give you and your colleagues an entirely fresh, new look at your customers but also something to share internally with other stakeholders in your organization. Personas are a component of the trail of logic that leads you to viable talk triggers.

Relentless Pursuit of Above Average

All these exercises and the knowledge you glean from them are designed to get you out of the data and into the day-to-day.

Anja Stas, CCO of the Flanders Meeting & Convention Center Antwerp (featured in chapter 10), summarizes the vital nature of remaining close to the customer: "It's the freaking basics of marketing. You don't start blabbing about how great you are . . . you start from walking in the shoes of your customer and you try to understand how you can make their lives better."

In the next chapter we'll show you how to create ideas that accomplish just that.

CHAPTER 15

Create Candidate Talk Triggers

Sure, you could just come up with a fun talk trigger idea and give it a whirl. But working with intent is always better than working with instinct alone. Plenty of well-meaning, possibly even great, ideas have faltered at the starting line because they didn't have the right context or fit.

Some big ideas failed but came back later. Pabst Blue Ribbon—lovingly known as PBR in hipster shorthand—had a tough couple of decades, beginning in the 1980s. Ted Wright, author of *Fizz* as well as the foreword to this book, engineered a comeback for the brand that celebrated its lack of pretense. From bike messenger races to Simpsons Pinball, PBR became an icon of a sort of everyday coolness. PBR's talk trigger was actually built around the interesting things its customers do every day. That wasn't a new approach for the company or a new marketing campaign. It's what PBR had been all along.

Other ideas struggled over time as they were copied. At one point

Hilton Garden Inn was among the market leaders with its customized beds, the Garden Sleep System. Now many hotels offer this amenity so it's no longer different.

Ideas do not always present themselves as clear winners or losers. Indeed, many inspired ideas seem like idiot ideas at first blush, but when examined further they begin to reveal their true genius.

This ambiguity illuminates the ongoing struggle everyone encounters. How do we separate great ideas from bad ideas? It's always easier to just go ahead and stick to the known things. We know that certain lead generation programs boost returns, that certain direct marketing efforts create resultant demand for our product, and that certain seasonal campaigns boost end-of-year volume reliably. Why not continue doing those?

It's worth reiterating an important point: Same is lame.

It's also worth reminding yourself: It's completely worth continuing to do those things.

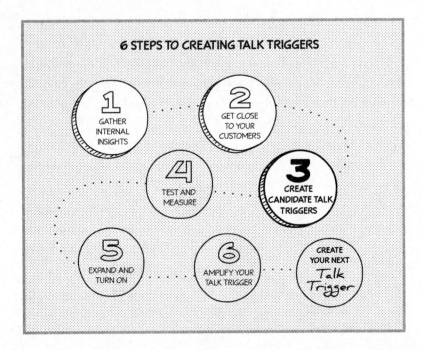

Talk trigger ideas are understandably challenging—and for good reason: They're different. But they're not, on their own, marketing. Done effectively, they generate marketing. Talk triggers are not campaigns, stunts, buzz marketing events, or influencer campaigns. So where do you begin?

Identify Potential Talk Triggers

Generating actual talk trigger ideas begins with revisiting all that you and your Triangle of Awesome team have learned in the previous two chapters.

In larger companies in which your talk trigger team is an actual group, you can do this by getting your Triangle of Awesome crew back together in a room, but this time with a different agenda and new insights. This may be the first time you've reassembled the group since your initial meeting.

For smaller companies in which one person wears many hats, *you* are the Triangle of Awesome—you may wish to do this as an exercise using sticky notes, but give yourself the advantage of spreading it out over a few different sessions. Write down your questions and answers, one per sticky note.

Whichever way you approach the actual work of organizing your insights, you are looking at questions we talked about in chapter 14:

- How do our customers experience our product?
- Why do our customers refer us today?
- What do our customers say about our brand, unaided?
- What do our customers say about our competitors or partners, unaided?
- Where in the product experience is the right time for us to introduce a talk trigger?

After examining your business from a customer's perspective, you may feel that you have a much better idea about how to answer those questions, and different members of your group will have varying perspectives.

This is fertile ground for talk trigger ideas—what comes out in the form of an insight, side note, or passing thought can indeed be the seed of an actual idea. Document them, and keep a note of the ideas even if they're not fully flushed out. You don't need much (if any) operational detail yet, just the seed of an idea.

ANSWER THESE QUESTIONS TO CREATE TALK TRIGGER IDEAS

So how do you generate talk trigger ideas, specifically?

Begin by reminding yourself and the group of the four *R*'s of talk triggers. They should be:

1. **Remarkable:** Something worth talking about
2. **Relevant:** Fits the context of your brand
3. **Reasonable:** Not a stunt or a "viral" idea
4. **Repeatable:** Available to all customers, not a select few on your VIP or influencer list

Then fill in the blanks. Literally. We created a worksheet for you with actual blanks; download it at TalkTriggers.com.

When you personally answer the following questions, answer as an actual customer. We've written them that way to help you frame it in your mind. Put yourself in your customers' shoes—perhaps a customer you've met or talked with, or think of a time you went through your own buyer's journey:

When I buy or use this product/service I'm . . .

What I don't expect from this product is . . .

What I'm talking about in my life right now is . . .
What I want is . . .
What I really want is . . .

These simple questions unlock most of the value from all the data, research, and customer conversations you've had since your first meeting. You may wish to add your own questions. The ideas you get here will surprise you!

Also try thinking about other elements of great ideas. For example, reconsider the five types of talk triggers (the 5 in our 4-5-6 system):

- Talkable empathy: The first type aligns your company's (or product's) values with your customers' values.
- Talkable usefulness: If it's the most useful example of the thing in your category, it's talkable.
- Talkable generosity: Doing something extra is talkable because, frankly, few others are willing to do so.
- Talkable speed: Speed is memorable and makes for great stories, especially today. People are busy!
- Talkable attitude: Are you able to be consistently unusual in your tone and tenor?

At this point in a meeting, you should have at least a handful of ideas. They might appear to be stupid and ridiculous on the surface, but as long as they meet the basic elements of a talk trigger (remarkable, relevant, reasonable, repeatable), don't erase them. At least not yet.

Plot Complexity

The last step to creating a candidate is all about prioritization.

If your organization is brand new to the whole concept of talk triggers, you need to be mindful of the value of incremental investment and opportunity cost. Yes, you could completely redesign your product to make it more remarkable, but you might not need to do that. And you certainly might struggle to gain traction internally to accomplish a major undertaking like that.

We like to plot talk trigger ideas on a grid to help guide both the initial test of an idea and the evolution of the concept in an organization. Many organizations have talk triggers that have evolved over time to reflect updated customer needs, new market realities, and competition. DoubleTree, with its cookies, didn't begin by offering warm cookies at check-in. It began as a hotel turndown service amenity and evolved as it became more popular and important to the brand.

To make it easier to visualize, we created a Complexity Map.

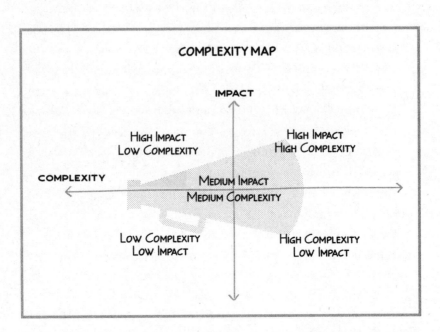

This map has two main variables: complexity and impact.

But before you go any further, you might want visual aids. Go to TalkTriggers.com and download a printable poster of this graphic.

Complexity is exactly what you'd think: How hard is this thing to pull off? It's vital to be realistic when you answer this question. A talk trigger that ends up being difficult to repeat may not pass a customer's sniff test, and it might fail to gain traction.

Impact, the other variable on our map, is going to be harder for you to know initially. If you've got a great idea for a talk trigger, simply asking your customers if they'd like it won't give you any actionable insight on its potential impact. That's because customers have difficulty visualizing things they haven't seen before; and because they've probably never thought about your proposed idea, they might not be able to tell you whether they'd be likely to share that story.

Yes, there are some ideas that will be obvious hits: Five Guys and its (almost endless) fries is a good example. But other ideas might be harder for customers to envision, like Graduate Hotels and its room keys.

So it's best to act incrementally, and the Complexity Map helps you to map the steps to accomplish that.

Take your list of ideas and have a brief discussion about the operational reality of each one. Can you accomplish this in a way that's repeatable?

You'll have some ideas that are easier to implement than others. That's actually ideal.

What you end up with are ideas plotted in one of four quadrants of the Complexity Map. Let's examine the strengths of each.

LOW IMPACT, LOW COMPLEXITY

These plotted ideas are very simple to execute but might not generate massive results. For example, if your idea is to use saltwater taffy instead of packing material, it'll definitely be noticed and probably generate some word of mouth. But it might not feel terribly talkable to the customer (even if you think it passes the test of the four *R*'s).

That being said, don't be too quick to prejudge the impact a particular talk trigger may have on your business. Just because it's easy does not mean it's low impact.

HIGH IMPACT, LOW COMPLEXITY

Five Guys Enterprises nails this category with its talk trigger and demonstrates precisely why it's vital you don't prejudge an idea's impact. The brand already makes fries—and lots of them. When it began adding extra fries to the bag, it knew nothing about the actual impact this would have on its business, but it's not surprising how much customers loved it. Now it's a talk trigger that keeps itself going and helps Five Guys differentiate its brand from competitors. It's the same talk trigger it's always been; the company is just reaping the rewards of being different.

HIGH IMPACT, HIGH COMPLEXITY

If something about an idea feels like it's trying too hard, you might want to follow your gut instinct. Inherent simplicity in any talk trigger is a beautiful thing. But if an idea you've generated is so complex that you fear consumers may not even understand it, perhaps revisit the concept.

Ideas in this category aren't immediate trash-can candidates. With some modification, they can actually become great ideas. Imagine if

Five Guys had an initial idea to add loads of chicken nuggets to every bag, even if customers hadn't ordered them.

First, Five Guys doesn't sell chicken nuggets. So that's a pretty obvious operational complexity. But customers would be stumped. It would likely generate a generous amount of word of mouth—who else would do that? Employees might not love the idea, feeling worried about the added operational complexity and the confusion it would likely lead to among customers.

With some modification, that chicken nugget idea becomes extra scoops of fries, and an incredibly complex idea becomes a really simple, really great idea.

Conversely, sometimes ideas in this category are so smart they're scary. If you've read Seth Godin's book *Purple Cow*, you might be familiar with his story about Dutch Boy paint. If not, here's the gist: Dutch Boy discovered that the real pain of paint was the can. The brand redesigned it and added a pourable spout to the can. Dutch Boy changed the entire category by introducing pourable paint cans.

Now, you might argue that changing the paint can is incredibly complex. Yes, it really is complex. But Dutch Boy has to put its paint in something.

Godin's summary of Dutch Boy's strategic brilliance: "It's so simple it's scary. They changed the can."

MEDIUM IMPACT, MEDIUM COMPLEXITY

Some companies are built to handle complexity better than others. And to be fair, complexity is a subjective measure: What one organization or company finds complex, others may revel in. Five Guys keeps its talk trigger simple, whereas Air New Zealand's is incredibly complex.

You might recall our story about Clube de Jornalistas from chapter 7. The staff gives every guest in their restaurant a gift when they leave, including cans of sardines. This approach might be considered a medium impact, medium complexity talk trigger. It's not operationally complicated but does require a bit more of its team than, say, Five Guys with its extra fries.

OVERCOME INTERNAL INERTIA

"We could never do that."

"It'd be impossible."

"Can you imagine what legal will have to say?"

It is very likely that Mark in legal will have things to say about your talk triggers. Also Ramona in purchasing. Likewise Frank in shipping, Alexa in sales, and the summer intern who inexplicably keeps asking where the fax machine is located even though his generation has supposedly never seen one.

Do you listen to them? Only if they have legitimate reasons to contribute their opinions.

What we've found over the years is something many employees and customers share: an inability to envision things that are different. Different is hard. Different can be an unfortunate reminder of the unimaginative side of human beings.

Fear is the most common reason that causes an obstacle to be thrown up in your path. Either the gatekeepers blocking your way are afraid the idea won't work, which might blow back on them, or they're worried that it will work and its success will somehow tarnish their reputation for creativity.

There are other obstacles, of course, than fear.

"WE DON'T HAVE THE BUDGET"

This is an easy one. No budget? Filter your talk trigger idea list for concepts that are free. Indeed, many talk triggers *are* free, or close to it. Does it actually cost Umpqua Bank any money to have a phone line directly connected to the CEO's office? It's a phone line. Phones already exist in the bank branch. Of course, Umpqua needed a special silver phone and a sign. But it's a marginal increase to an existing line item.

Does it cost money for Graduate Hotels to create talkable room keys? Barely. It already has to make room keys. Now it just makes different ones.

If cost is the major stumbling block for your organization, search your list for talk trigger ideas that fit this model: Take something you already do and already pay for, and try to do it differently. This strategy typically shuts down any concern about runaway spending.

The expense of doing something can also be an argument IN your favor. Remember when we talked about Skip's Kitchen in chapter 10? Skip Wahl gives away ample amounts of free food. Every time someone draws a joker, the meal is on the house. That talk trigger generates considerable word of mouth—enough that he has never spent a single dollar on advertising.

Saving money isn't something anyone has ever complained about, particularly if the person began the conversation by saying, "But we don't have the money." You're right, we don't!

"WE CAN'T MEASURE IT"

Well, it's actually very true: Word of mouth is not easy to measure. So much of it happens offline, outside the reaches of any measurement instrument, that it feels unknowable. If ninety-eight people mentioned your bakery at a holiday party last weekend, you might have seen a pickup in business, but you might not have noticed it or thought to ask where people heard about you.

As with many undertakings, talk triggers need methodical planning to be measured effectively. One common way is to ask the simple question we often forget: "How did you hear about us?" If you're measuring the responses, have tested a talk trigger, and see a spike in the "I heard about you from a friend or family member" category, you can safely correlate your idea to an outcome.

The challenge with correlation and causation is certain to create a headache for at least one of your peers, perhaps even for you as you struggle to understand how to value what you've built in a talk trigger. We're going to look at measurement in more detail in the next chapter and give you some specific techniques. For now, when dealing with this particular bit of critique, remind your colleague (or yourself) that talk triggers are measurable, just not perhaps in the ways you're used to. The case studies in this book might give you a specific example to keep in your back pocket. If it works for The Cheesecake Factory, WindsorONE Lumber, FreshBooks, Double-Tree by Hilton, and countless others, you'll find a way to make it work for you.

"IT'S TOO COMPLICATED"

There is validity to this concern, and it may indicate you need to revisit the Complexity Map again. Some ideas may turn out to be more operationally complex than others, and in the course of due diligence, you need to listen to that counsel.

Often the spirit behind this comment is one of frustration about change; it may not actually be complicated, just different.

"WHAT IF THEY DON'T LIKE IT?"

The answer to this question is easy: Nobody will talk about it. You won't see any lift anywhere, and you can find another idea. But what if they love it?

This question is more about corporate culture than curiosity.

Some companies have been so reliant on marketing expenditure that it becomes difficult to embrace a different reality.

In chapter 1 we cited the very real distinction between The Cheesecake Factory and Darden Restaurants (operators of Olive Garden, the Capital Grille, Yard House, and more). The Cheese-cake Factory, one of the brands with the strongest word of mouth in the restaurant business, spends 0.20 percent of total sales on advertising. Darden Restaurants, in contrast, spends almost $270 million more per year.

The culture of the two companies is very different. Yours may be less receptive to a wide-armed embrace of talk triggers today. Begin small and build trust. You'll get there.

Now that you have candidate talk triggers, it's time to determine just how impactful and effective they are in catalyzing conversations among your customers. In the next chapter we'll show you how to test and measure operational differentiators.

CHAPTER 16

Test and Measure Your Talk Triggers

Things that take time to grow inherently invite skeptics. We're so used to quick results—particularly in marketing—that it feels almost unnatural to intentionally slow down.

It's not unlike making Thanksgiving dinner using ingredients you planted during the summer. Slowly and carefully throughout the months you picked the weeds and warded off pests intent on their own premature feast until the time was just right to fetch fruits from the tree and vegetables from their vines. It's slow and methodical, but it leaves a lasting impression.

The reality is that talk triggers invite skeptics. After all, if word of mouth was *so* obvious and equally easy to observe, this book wouldn't have much purpose.

But it's not that talk triggers are actually *hard* to measure, because they're not. It's that they're hard to measure in ways in which

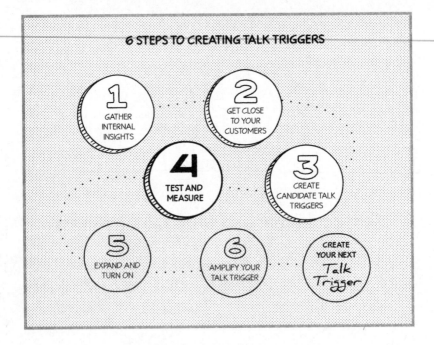

6 STEPS TO CREATING TALK TRIGGERS

you and, more vitally, the naysayers in your organization are historically accustomed. By definition, word of mouth takes time to flower because it relies on *one* customer telling one other potential customer (or a few) about you.

Word of mouth, however, is more persuasive and effective at the individual level because real, trusted people make recommendations to other real people.

While the real-life-experience nature of word of mouth is what makes it work, ironically, the corresponding lack of immediacy is what many potential practitioners find frustrating.

You do need to allow talk triggers time to work. When faced with impatient skeptics in your organization, you need to understand where they're coming from. Yes, it's possible they're bad apples, but generally they're concerned about investments that scale. So change the conversation. Make it about the method, not the timeline. The good news is that your success horizon is not dictated by a campaign or a media buy, but rather by the steady growth inherent in word of mouth. Steady growth is a scalable thing, because it requires no further investment from your organization. It happens organically. But to accomplish it, you have to begin slowly and build to a crescendo of effectiveness.

It's also incredibly important to recognize that even if you believe you've created the ultimate talk trigger, your customers may disagree. After all, you are not in their shoes. You know *way* more about your product or service than they do, and what resonates for you in your office may not ring their bell in the same way.

This potential for cognitive bias is why it's imperative that you don't decide on a viable talk trigger only in your planning process and then roll it out and wait to claim victory. Because what if it doesn't work? What if it isn't remarkable enough to stimulate conversation? It is imperative to test and measure your candidate talk trigger first, to better ensure that it will have the desired effect on your customers.

You know how some guy ten thousand years ago said, "Hey, we should eat this avocado." Or some gal had asked, "What if we figured out a way to take all these dangerous and poisonous spines out? I bet this sea urchin would taste amazing!" You are those people. You are a pioneer, feeling your way along until you hit on your own genius word-of-mouth idea.

At the testing and measurement stage, it's important to embrace the experimental nature of potential talk triggers instead of running from the lack of certainty.

Test versus Measure: Two Mind-sets

There are two distinct mind-sets that we'll explore in this chapter.

The first is the testing mind-set: How do you know your idea is good enough to sustain its own word of mouth? One way you'll know it's working sounds a lot like the answer to a question posed in a corny 1980s rom-com: How do you know you're in love?

"You'll just feel it."

It's a warm, fuzzy feeling that overcomes you. It just . . . works.

Not satisfied with that logic? Admittedly, it can be difficult to manage this stuff by gut feeling alone. Maybe you had a big lunch—a food baby—or an extra cup of morning coffee is leaving your gut feeling extra warm.

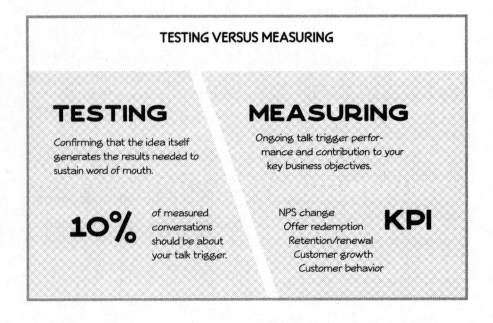

TESTING VERSUS MEASURING

TESTING

Confirming that the idea itself generates the results needed to sustain word of mouth.

10% of measured conversations should be about your talk trigger.

MEASURING

Ongoing talk trigger performance and contribution to your key business objectives.

NPS change
Offer redemption
Retention/renewal
Customer growth
Customer behavior

KPI

Let's try something with numbers instead. It's less romantic—unless data gives you a warm, fuzzy feeling.

What we learned in our research for DoubleTree by Hilton Hotels and Resorts and The Cheesecake Factory helps us to establish a baseline benchmark for talk trigger performance.

When you compile conversation in all the venues we're about to recommend, look at the percentage of conversation that's related to talk triggers versus other topics about your business or brand.

It's a simple equation: For optimal performance, a talk trigger should be present in at least 25 percent of the conversations. Talk triggers for both DoubleTree and The Cheesecake Factory feature in approximately 35 percent of the conversations about these brands. But our research suggests that not all brands need to get to that number for talk triggers to be effective; one-quarter of customer conversations will keep it going efficiently.

Your initial test of a talk trigger idea may not mature to a 25 percent threshold in the limited space of time you allowed to kick its tires. When this happens we advocate for a smaller percentage that suggests the potential for growth and success. In the short term, 10 percent of customer conversation is a good place to begin. If you cannot encourage 10 percent of your test audience to begin talking about your trigger voluntarily, it is clearly not the right mechanism to incite conversation. Perhaps it's not novel enough, or hasn't been perceived as unique by your customers. You'll need to retool and try again.

We'll summarize this again for you for reference purposes:

- As a sprint test during a limited period of time, you should be seeing evidence of your trigger in at least 10 percent of conversations.
- As an endurance test, over time and once made permanent, a talk trigger should be present in 25 percent of your customer conversations.

Test Talk Triggers

Before we discuss the art and science of ongoing talk trigger measurement, remember that we are in the testing stage of the process. We're not in full eye-popping Microsoft Excel measurement dashboard just yet.

You've probably assembled your ideas into a prioritized list of high potentials. Do you have a good idea? How good? It's very difficult to know whether a talk trigger will work without putting it into the hands of customers to see how they respond to it (or don't).

Unless you have the benefit of being a small business that can just do the thing, giving it a whirl to see how people respond, you'll probably need an actual test to see whether it generates results. How do you test a talk trigger?

Your testing protocol will depend on what business you are in and how that business is structured. We'll look at a few examples here that demonstrate different ways of testing a talk trigger for different businesses that will be helpful as you frame the testing plan for your own idea.

AN ONLINE SOFTWARE COMPANY

FreshBooks chose live customer dinners as its initial talk trigger, and that created a nice opening for testing: Because the meals were hosted by traveling FreshBooks employees, they were by design segmented by geography. An idea like this is optimally designed for testing and measurement, because you can look at the customer feedback that was emailed in or shared with associates during calls, social media chatter, and even customer survey data all sliced up by location.

If you operate exclusively online, think about how you can replicate this logic and apply it toward testing your talk trigger. Can you limit the initial availability of your talk trigger to a specific customer segment that is easily measured?

A LOCAL MERCHANT

In total contrast with exclusively online companies, local businesses face a real customer segmentation challenge: If all your customers live in the same city, then how do you withhold talk triggers from some of them, yet still offer them, but only to a specific segment of your customers?

It's not a good idea to exclude customers. You may want to consider testing by time instead and making very specific choices about the testing method. Send out a customer feedback survey prior to testing your talk trigger, for example, and then try it out for a pre-defined period of time (one week? a month?). That's up to you—and then do another customer feedback survey. Bolster your findings with some social media listening and you'll have a good idea of how your talk trigger performed.

A PROFESSIONAL SERVICES COMPANY

What do locksmiths and oral surgeons have in common?

When you need them, sometimes you need them urgently. You don't fit standard customer segmentation. You go through the typical marketing funnel—those categories of awareness, consideration, intent, and purchase—within minutes. How can you begin to measure a talk trigger in that environment?

We're advocates of what we call the ABL mind-set—always be listening. Even the most rudimentary of social media, online, review, or email-support software can sort topics by date, giving you a tangible set of data against which to compare any talk trigger effort that you might decide to test.

Are you a dentist who wants to try free fifteen-minute chair massages for your patients after their appointment? Great! Please let us know so we can make an appointment. And be sure to compare discussion topics before and after to see whether your talk trigger did indeed create customer conversation.

How about a tax prep business? If your business has natural peaks and valleys, like many in the tax prep industry, it can be difficult to segment anything by time. When you're busy you're busy, and when you're not the volume tapers off.

In these cases, you may not have any data to use as a comparison. Therefore, you'll probably want to examine active conversation just during the time you offered the talk trigger, analyzing its topic and sentiment. Did people notice your talk trigger, and did they mention it? Remind yourself, as a test, you're looking to see whether at least 10 percent of conversations mention your talk trigger.

The Observer Effect

As you explore the various ways you can test a talk trigger, it's essential to think through the method you'll use to study and measure them. Not all measurement methods give you reliable and actionable insights. Sometimes the method used can itself create the illusion of success for a talk trigger simply by the way it is designed.

For example, asking your customers directly if they'd be likely to share a talk trigger idea before they actually experience it is probably not going to generate meaningful insights. It might even raise suspicion or alarm among customers and cause them to think you've lost your mind.

You cannot measure things in this manner because how you measure things can alter how it's perceived. Offering a customer a talk trigger and measuring its success has to remain separate. The measurement needs to be invisible to the customer or you'll end up with data that doesn't reflect their propensity to share the trigger.

In physics this is known as the "observer effect." It behaves a bit like this: Measuring the air pressure in a tire with a pressure gauge in and of itself impacts the air pressure in the tire. That small release of air disrupts the state of the thing being measured.

In a similar way, measuring a talk trigger is tricky: If a customer thinks that what you're up to is inauthentic and they feel like you're trying to track their use of it, it's going to sour them on the experience.

Think about it this way: How would *you* react if you were offered any of the talk triggers in this book, and immediately were asked by the company if you noticed and were going to mention it?

Your goal is to observe the environment of conversation about your talk trigger, rather than influence how it behaves.

Measure Talk Triggers

When you've confirmed that an idea has sufficiently grabbed hold and meets the 10 percent test (or even better, the 25 percent long-term threshold) we outlined above in "Test versus Measure: Two Mindsets," you're ready to move on to a more thorough measurement plan for the talk trigger. This sets you up for a broad deployment of the talk trigger.

A standard playbook of metrics and KPIs (key performance indicators) might offer you only tangential evidence of success rather than illuminating the full impact of your triggers. A big part of that reason lies in the inherent measurement challenge with word of mouth: A lot of it happens offline. But that's the part you need to understand best because, over time, it's where your most reliable sort of customer referrals thrive.

Because of the split nature of online versus offline word of mouth, your measurement instruments need to reflect that disparity. To

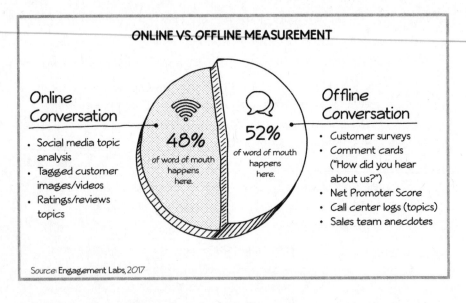

ONLINE VS. OFFLINE MEASUREMENT

Online Conversation

- Social media topic analysis
- Tagged customer images/videos
- Ratings/reviews topics

48% of word of mouth happens here.

52% of word of mouth happens here.

Offline Conversation

- Customer surveys
- Comment cards ("How did you hear about us?")
- Net Promoter Score
- Call center logs (topics)
- Sales team anecdotes

Source: Engagement Labs, 2017

fully understand the value of your talk trigger, you need to be examining both online and offline conversations.

This should be done with a combination of primary research directly fielded to your customers in the form of surveys and comment cards as well as social media topic analysis. Looking at offline data—call center logs, email-support software topic analysis, and sales team interviews—will help you to see the full reality for your talk trigger. It gives the full perspective of the likelihood for someone to share the talk trigger story.

Kill Your Darlings

Even amazing talk trigger ideas can be remarkably fragile. They don't benefit from durability until your customers begin talking about them, and they don't get to that point quickly. How soon is too soon to say sayonara to an idea?

Decide ahead of time what those thresholds are going to be for your business. You already know that talk triggers don't always work quickly. There is risk in deploying an idea and waiting for it to work. There is, after all, a difference between hope and reality. The reason it's helpful to test an idea with a small segment of your customer base is community insight. Like a virus, things catch on faster in a small community than they do in a large one. Niche ideas that have an opportunity to grow out of their shells might help you to get some solid footing.

How long do you have to wait to draw conclusions?

Not all ideas are created equal in their ability to show results quickly. If you recall the ideas from the Complexity Map in chapter 15, some of them have long run-up periods. If you're adding extra fries to a bag of takeout, like Five Guys, you'll probably see results quickly. If you're taking time to call patients in advance of their appointments to see you, like Dr. Glenn Gorab, it might take several weeks or more before you see any real measurable feedback.

For simple ideas that are easier to implement, give your idea at least a couple of weeks. For ideas further along that Complexity Map, it will be necessary to wait at least thirty to forty-five days before examining key metrics. Naturally, some customer segments and community types will demonstrate traction faster.

There may also be cases in which you and/or your team are convinced that you have a great idea and many customers are responding to it, but it's not quite reaching the 25 percent threshold. In this case, you might find that making minor adjustments to the idea is all that's needed to unlock its potential.

Go back to your original research—gathered when you began this process (outlined in chapter 13)—and discuss as a group what modifications might help strengthen the four R's case: remarkable, relevant, reasonable, and repeatable.

When that's done and you still come up short, you'd be wise to kill your darlings and scrap the idea rather than to deploy and test another one.

Keep tabs on your progress! Once you reach the percent target in the testing phase—10 percent at minimum—and you've established some ongoing measurement KPIs, you'll have a good candidate for a permanent talk trigger. We'll review this in the next chapter.

CHAPTER 17

Expand and Turn On

There are cases where talk triggers inherently assume a starring role in an organization. The Cheesecake Factory's book-length menu is a shining example of this, taking center stage alongside the huge selection of actual cheesecake flavors that diners pass en route to their tables.

Not all organizations have the appetite for endless menus and dozens of dessert flavors. Talk triggers can also be smaller and subtle, so interwoven that they can be mistaken for the actual product. Americollect's talk trigger—Ridiculously Nice Collections—reflects that style. And others are small, stand-alone efforts, like Graduate Hotels with its remarkable room keys.

We've talked about how you can create talk triggers that have different components, some easier to launch and test than others. If you've now tested your talk trigger and find that it's meeting your stated objectives (at least a 10 percent conversation threshold), it's time to expand it and make it available to your entire customer base.

Because talk triggers are designed to be operational differentiators rather than marketing campaigns, how you think about expanding it to your entire company needs to reflect a different deployment model than marketing programs. We'll talk in the next chapter about how to amplify your talk trigger by using more traditional elements of the marketing mix, but let's focus now on how you can get others in the company excited about what you've built.

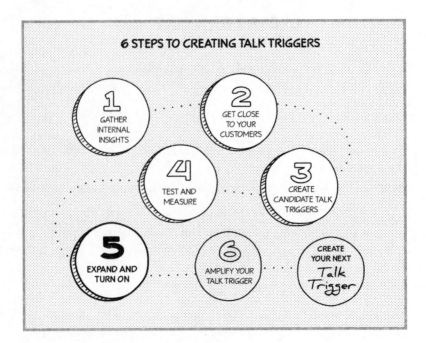

6 STEPS TO CREATING TALK TRIGGERS

1. GATHER INTERNAL INSIGHTS
2. GET CLOSE TO YOUR CUSTOMERS
3. CREATE CANDIDATE TALK TRIGGERS
4. TEST AND MEASURE
5. EXPAND AND TURN ON
6. AMPLIFY YOUR TALK TRIGGER

CREATE YOUR NEXT Talk Trigger

How to Scale a Talk Trigger

So far, you've been in test mode, seeking differentiators that generate momentum on their own. Now that you've identified and refined your talk trigger, you need to redouble your rollout efforts. What good is a talk trigger if nobody talks about it?

Remember that talk triggers are not marketing. Thus, the ideas you might use to support a new marketing campaign—those elements of paid, owned, and earned media (POEM)—should not be your first stop on the launch train for word of mouth.

Instead, we recommend a different framework that we call SEE. It stands for stakeholders, employees, and enterprise.

The Talk Trigger SEE Framework

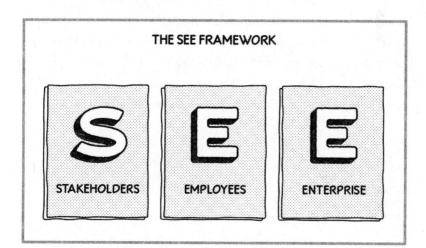

THE SEE FRAMEWORK

S   E   E

STAKEHOLDERS   EMPLOYEES   ENTERPRISE

The core element of a talk trigger is the story it creates. Remember, this is how talk triggers are different from USPs (unique selling propositions). Talk triggers are about *stories*. USPs are about *bullet points*.

Your talk triggers story might be rooted in humanity, like Jay Sofer at Lockbusters and his passion for animal welfare.

Or you might find your story is rooted in the celebration of the unique nature of your customers, like FreshBooks and its live customer dinners and events.

But the reality is that even if your customers LOVE your talk trigger, it will never work unless everyone in your organization—large and small—is equally smitten. This need to get everyone in the firm pulling on the same rope is particularly and egregiously true for word of mouth. If marketing does some sort of short-term promotion, it's not necessary that the rest of the company BELIEVE in it, or even know about it in some cases. But word of mouth is very different because talk triggers are born from operations-level differentiators, not slogans and ads. You have to BE different to convince customers that you are worthy of conversation. And being different requires every person and every department to align around the talk trigger.

It's like jazz. The musicians have the freedom to do their own thing, but always within the framework of the overall initiative. In their case, the song. In yours, the desire to get your current customers telling their friends about why you are noteworthy.

Let's look at the SEE framework for expanding talk triggers and gaining organization alignment. The first group is the stakeholders.

STAKEHOLDERS

Different organizations have different stakeholders, but we generally think of them as internal and external in nature. Internal stakeholders are people who work for and with you; we'll talk about them next. For now, when we use the word *stakeholders*, we mean those who are external to your organization. Suppliers, contractors, vendors, partners, board members, and community advocates are all examples of stakeholders.

Why might a stakeholder be interested in and want to learn about your talk trigger?

Because it's interesting, unique, and different. If it works for you, it will probably benefit them as well. They're associated with your organization and likely eager to have a reason to talk about it. The talk trigger gives them a reason to speak up and share a story or anecdote. A quick agenda item or email update is probably enough to get the point across to most stakeholders and give them the context they need. The next time they hear about your (online or offline) talk trigger, they can speak up and say, "I know, isn't that cool? I love that they do that."

In certain cases, one of your identified stakeholder groups might be a beneficiary of your talk trigger, as is the case with Jay Sofer and Lockbusters. He donates his customer tips to Sugar Mutts Rescue, turning the animal shelter into one of his talk trigger stakeholders.

EMPLOYEES

Employees, like external stakeholders, love to share stories. A unique talk trigger can become a point of pride for every employee and give employees their own version of the story to share. Perhaps the delivery of the talk trigger is something unique and helps to provide an insider's perspective on the culture of the company.

For certain, if your own team members do not find your talk trigger worthy of conversation, there is *no way* your customers will. Your greatest word-of-mouth advocates have to be your existing employees.

Clearly articulate to employees why you've selected this talk trigger and how they're involved in the story. Don't announce it only in an email. Make everyone feel like they are co-owners of this differentiator, because, after all, they are the ones who have to live up to it every day.

Think about Skip at Skip's Kitchen. It was his idea to give away a free meal if customers pulled a joker when asked to pick a card. He began the talk trigger when he worked the counter himself, subsequently training other team members how to do it with maximum chatter impact. He didn't just announce "do this, starting tomorrow" in a staff meeting.

You have to LIVE your talk trigger in every sense. Every team member at DoubleTree by Hilton is massively tuned in to the uniqueness and power of the cookie giveaway at check-in. It's part of the company's DNA.

ENTERPRISE

Inconsistent execution of a talk trigger will lead to its eventual decline and death. A good talk trigger applied haphazardly chips at one of the core elements that make talk triggers work: They're repeatable. If your talk trigger is too hard to execute, or is allowed to become optional, it won't be consistently repeated and will devolve into a random surprise and delight stunt.

If Five Guys gave inconsistent amounts of extra fries with each order, the story would move from "Wow, this is *a lot* of fries!" to "Geez, I got a lot more fries last time!" Inconsistency is one way you move from a positive talk trigger to a negative one.

How can you ensure a consistent application of the talk trigger everywhere? Look at the entire enterprise. For Five Guys, more fries means more potatoes (they're hand cut in every location). That means Five Guys needs to order and store those potatoes. Five Guys also needs to train thousands of employees to deliver extra fries with every order, every time.

Beyond the actual provision of the trigger itself, you may need to think more broadly about how your talk trigger is supported across your business. Are the FAQs on your website reflective of the trigger? Do you need to update customer service scripts or internal processes to better ensure that they're consistent?

Graduate Hotels, with its customized room keys, needs to invent and print a different room key design for every hotel location. That certainly impacts the people on the team tasked with that job.

For Americollect, with its Ridiculously Nice Collections, the talk trigger is less a tangible thing and more a persistent culture. In this case, it needs to build into its hiring and onboarding systems clear processes to screen for and educate new team members that it is a *very* different type of collections company.

The SEE (stakeholders, employees, and enterprise) framework will help you nail all four criteria that have to be met for a differentiator to be a talk trigger: It shall be remarkable, relevant, reasonable, and repeatable.

Now let's look at how you build unstoppable internal momentum for your talk trigger and expand its reach.

Expand Your Talk Trigger

Most organizations with strong talk triggers go through some necessary evolution. It's pretty rare that you identify a talk trigger, roll it out, and find that it works at full speed from day one. Skip's Kitchen, for example, is the exception. It's not usually quite that seamless.

The methods we've prescribed for you so far have helped you and your organization to get back in front of customers and think about what their needs are, and also how a talk trigger might give your customers a clear and present reason to share their experience. Armed with actual data, you'll have all the tools you need to address the internal "it can't be done" and "we could never" resistance that all organizations experience. That friction feels like heavy grit sandpaper on any creative mind, slowly grinding away any signs of optimism.

All the knowledge you've gained about the talk triggers process so far has remained within the confines of your Triangle of Awesome. It's time to do some show-and-tell with your colleagues, sharing your talk triggers experience and its impact on your business. This is where you help your peers escape the operational funk and begin to think creatively about the business again.

Build a Coalition

What's the easiest way to get your peers to pay attention to an email meeting request? Try this for your meeting subject line: How we get more customers for free.

Who would not attend that meeting? It's going to create intrigue and possibly some stink eyes from the seriously skeptical. But you'll have the data you need, along with a coalition of peers from your Triangle of Awesome talk triggers team. Use that meeting invitation to seed some intrigue, then deliver the punch line in the meeting: "We discovered a way to inspire our current customers to bring us more customers."

With a bit of snark someone will ask the obvious: How?

And with that question comes an opening to share the talk triggers story with your peers. Tell them about what you learned from the customer research and what the experience was like to live in the shoes of your customers and get into their minds. Next, share the initial idea or set of ideas that you tested. Tell your peers candidly about how the idea(s) performed. Share the results it has generated for the business, even in the testing phase, so they understand the context of how talk triggers behave and generate outcomes.

Then say, "We're just getting started." Give several examples of companies that you admire that have large or operationally complex talk triggers. Some of those examples are in this book—The

Cheesecake Factory, DoubleTree by Hilton Hotels and Resorts, and Five Guys Enterprises.

You'll see wheels begin to turn.

If you feel like you've got the opening and interest, share your Complexity Map from chapter 15 mapped with the ideas you generated. Highlight the ideas that you tested and how they performed, but then talk about the other ideas that are further along the complexity spectrum.

What you could end up with is a willingness to get along and test new ideas, as well as a collection of commitments from peers who would otherwise be pure skeptics. You might generate a handful of concepts that evolve a current talk trigger into other aspects of the customer experience.

Find an Executive Champion

A successful talk triggers deployment might also result in another helpful side effect: to produce an executive champion.

The insights uncovered during a talk triggers trial can have widespread impact.

Sean Ellis, now the CEO of GrowthHackers, had this experience at LogMeIn with its Rescue product, a remote support tool that enables its users to access their computer no matter where they are. Early on in his time at the company, Sean discovered a gap in the customer onboarding experience that led to customers dropping off and not remaining active.

Addressing that gap itself was not a talk trigger, but because the company relied heavily on word of mouth for customer growth and acquisition, it was a clear and present danger. Even after presenting and discussing the issues with the product team, LogMeIn couldn't find a resolution. Its product team was focused on other things.

Indeed, the issues were not exclusively product related, and Sean knew that. It was also marketing and related to web design.

Intent on driving forward to a solution, Sean prepared some data for the company's CEO and shared his findings and concerns along with a suggested resolution for fixing the challenges. The CEO agreed with the data and launched a unified effort across the company to reimagine customer onboarding. Because of that renewed company-wide focus, LogMeIn found that 80 percent of new customers were acquired via word of mouth.

That narrow opening to an executive champion might be all that's needed to harness his or her full support behind taking your talk triggers to the major league.

Data isn't the only thing that a CEO or CMO (chief marketing officer) might want to know before they put their full weight behind a talk trigger. Spend some time thinking through the story you'll share. Ted Wright outlined a useful, old-school method in *Fizz*, one that has the added benefit of food.

He takes his staff out to a meal for a little role-play. Each employee is assigned a role or a persona and then practices telling his or her story. Why is this approach useful? It makes you think about how someone will actually share your story.

"The point is to nail down the words and phrases you will use when you tell your CMO that you want to try some word-of-mouth marketing. Before you can tackle questions of budget and ROI [return on investment], you need to be able to convince him or her that this whole thing makes sense."

This method can be remarkably useful for smaller companies. If you're in a situation where you find yourself assuming the role of CEO, COO, CMO, CTO, and CFO—as is the case with so many small businesses—a simple, casual exercise during a meal with colleagues like Wright does might be the thing that generates momentum and internal excitement.

Gain Internal Momentum

Just as in physics, managing any organization successfully is all about momentum. Talk triggers are one path to reinvigorating virtually any organization when it feels like momentum might be in short supply. When customers, employees, and other stakeholders are excited, everyone feels excited.

As your talk trigger grows its internal fan base, be sure to share early wins. When something amazing happens—a new growth threshold is met or a sales target is blown out of the water—celebrate it and remind everyone that the customer is the reason why. It feels great to be different!

Effective talk triggers create great brand experiences, and these small internal celebrations can reinforce how meaningful a talk trigger is to your organization's esprit de corps.

Because they survive beyond campaigns and stunts, talk triggers are durable and lead to an excellent ongoing narrative for your organization. It's a sort of endurance marketing.

We've reviewed testing, measuring, and activating your talk trigger. Now how do you get people actually talking about it at scale? Next we'll look at amplifying your talk trigger.

CHAPTER 18

Amplify Your Talk Trigger

You've identified a remarkable idea worth talking about. How do you get customers talking about your talk trigger? If you passed the initial 10 percent test but are not quite at that 25 percent threshold of conversations, do you just sit and wait?

There are things you can do to spark conversation and generate momentum, but remember that a talk trigger by definition is a strategic operational differentiator. It's not a customer referral program or an influencer campaign.

Naturally, one of the outcomes of great talk triggers—and true for every example in this book—is this: They generate chatter and referrals. So what separates a talk trigger from a referral program?

Many companies offer referral programs. Often customers are rewarded with something for free or receive a temporary discount on monthly service, or even get a T-shirt. Can you name the last

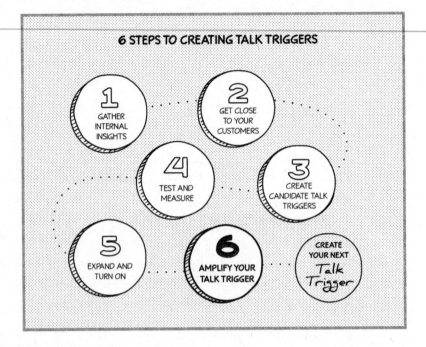

6 STEPS TO CREATING TALK TRIGGERS

1 GATHER INTERNAL INSIGHTS

2 GET CLOSE TO YOUR CUSTOMERS

3 CREATE CANDIDATE TALK TRIGGERS

4 TEST AND MEASURE

5 EXPAND AND TURN ON

6 AMPLIFY YOUR TALK TRIGGER

CREATE YOUR NEXT Talk Trigger

time that an incentive like that actually caused you to refer friends, family, or colleagues to something?

Perhaps you can think of an example, or even two, but it's probably safe for us to assume that it's unusual.

Why? Because people aren't billboards.

Or, as Jonah Berger wrote in *Contagious*, "People don't seem to like walking advertisements."

Talk triggers work because they're subtle and tangible. They're not designed as quid pro quo referral devices, delivered in exchange for the email addresses of friends and family.

They're genuine experiences, not advertising. This is the precise reason that a word-of-mouth impression drives five times more sales than advertising. But word of mouth and advertising are not mutually exclusive, as we've established. Each assists the other, and in this chapter we'll examine how you can (and should) use your marketing mix to support your talk triggers.

Set the Stage for Simplicity

You just might have a fan willing to tattoo your logo on his nether regions, but most businesses are not that lucky.

What are the messages and stories that consumers are willing to share? They're easy to understand and interpret. In other words, they're usually free of asterisks, conditions, and legalese. It turns out customers don't like terms and conditions, particularly when they're telling a story.

"Let me tell you about this great hotel! They welcome you with a warm chocolate chip cookie, quantities limited and may not be available in all locations." These words are probably rarely spoken by a customer with much enthusiasm.

This is just not how people share stories. Your talk trigger message has to be crisp, concise, and simple. There cannot be exceptions, caveats, or circumstances.

Holiday World takes this approach very seriously with its unlimited soda offer. Many theme and amusement parks sell some form of reusable cup that includes unlimited refills. Lose the cup and you lose your drink refill privileges. It has conditions that make it feel contractual rather than remarkable.

Holiday World has a different approach, as we've explored: Soda is always free, every day of the year. You don't need a special cup; free cups are at the drink station. And even in the restaurants. There is no fee. No limit. All ages. And that makes it so easy to amplify across its marketing mix, as the talkable generosity message is simple and easy to communicate.

"It's not just an investment; it's a communications strategy too. We put it in all of our advertisements. We post it on social media. We make sure that we let people know that's something that we do. Thunderbird is the most fantastic ride on the planet, but I would push free soft drinks over that any day of the week if I was trying to tell a guest why they should come here," said Paula Werne, director of communications.

Another way to think about this is by asking the following: Can you explain your talk trigger to a child? If you cannot, it's going to be hard to effectively amplify for both your customers and your marketing efforts.

That should be your first step in this stage: Explain the talk trigger to a child, and if the child gets it, then you can explore how to amplify and promote it.

One of our own talk triggers for this book is a free presentation about the power of talk triggers and word of mouth that we invite you to download and present to team members inside your business. You can easily customize it to talk about your own talk trigger. It's totally free at TalkTriggers.com.

Create Your "Because" Statement

Somewhere in the life cycle of any talk trigger a decision was made: A specific thing is being done for a reason. Perhaps the ideas you developed and mapped on the Complexity Map all tied back to your company mission or your community. There's a reason for every talk trigger.

It's vital that you make that story known to people. It's much, much easier for someone to insert themselves into story, and that's critical for the success of your talk trigger. The story does not need to be complex or overwrought. In fact, the simpler the better.

DoubleTree by Hilton gives guests a warm chocolate chip cookie at check-in because it wants them to feel welcome.

Five Guys gives more fries because it wants customers to feel like they got something extra.

Performers Penn and Teller greet every guest after a show because they want guests to feel like they are part of a community.

What's your "because" statement?

Complete this sentence: We do [TALK TRIGGER] because [REASON].

A story helps to make your talk trigger more personal. If you've decided that you'll make donations a part of your talk trigger, let people know where and why.

If you redesigned your product to make it more comfortable, as Air New Zealand did with the Skycouch, let people know it's because you realize travel has become uncomfortable.

Your brand's "because" is the link most people need to translate your talk trigger into a story they can become part of and share with their friends, family, and colleagues. Their experience, by extension, becomes part of your talk trigger.

Amplify Your Talk Trigger in Your Marketing Mix

Your marketing mix is the launching point for amplifying your talk trigger.

As Holiday World does with its free beverages, you want to look for opportunities to share that element of the customer experience in other media environments, including the following:

- Advertising
- Social media
- Customer service responses
- Email campaigns
- Website

Many of the people we talked to for this book reflected on the benefits their talk triggers had on their paid media efforts. Double-Tree actually launched an advertising campaign around its talk trigger, dubbed the #SweetWelcome. Its objective for supporting its talk trigger with paid media stems from a change in travel behavior, particularly among younger travelers.

"Hospitality marketing continues to evolve for a new generation of travelers," said Stuart Foster, Hilton VP of global brand marketing. "It's no longer enough to develop integrated marketing campaigns focused solely on the 'hard product,' such as on-site food and beverage offerings or new bathroom amenities."

It's worth noting the importance for a talk trigger to stand on its own in the absence of any other media support. But as we've noted in this chapter and elsewhere, the benefits do create a sort of Venn diagram of goodwill in a number of areas of the business. Advertising, social media, and paid media are some of those beneficiaries.

Media and Influencers

Doing something just for the attention it gets you might land you a reality series—but it won't win you many long-term fans. Media interest is a side effect of great talk triggers, not a goal.

How should you handle marketing your talk trigger to reporters and other influencers? Very carefully.

We'd advocate that you actually don't do any outreach about it. It's an effective talking point that differentiates your company and sets it apart from the competition. Use it in your key messaging architecture and as a proof point showing your company's customer commitment.

Beyond that, talk triggers are best left to their intended audience: your customers.

Evolving Your Operations

Ever been to a Krispy Kreme when the red light was on? You will never look at a doughnut the same way again. All freestanding Krispy Kreme donut locations have a neon sign outside that says HOT NOW when the donuts are coming down the world's tastiest assembly line. This very visual cue alerts passersby that the time for doughnuts has drawn nigh and that an unplanned stop will yield pillowy, delicious rewards.

That's the pinnacle of talk trigger amplification: It becomes part of the product. At Krispy Kreme, amplification of the trigger (fresh, hot doughnuts!) is so important, the company also created a dedicated app to alert doughnutseekers to the nearest warm morsel.

It's also the most advanced and complicated to execute operationally. Can you get to this stage? Yes, of course you can. That's a longer-term mission and not something you'll have the data or clarity to create straight out of the gate. Take smaller steps en route and you'll discover you've built something durable along the way to building ideas that are the size and scope of Krispy Kreme's.

Guidelines for Amplifying

Talk triggers are difficult to get right. But when you do, do yourself a favor: Don't bury the lead in pursuit of subtlety. Being too subtle about your talk trigger is as detrimental as being too promotional with it.

One example of a company that could possibly benefit from making a talk trigger more pronounced is Amazon, specifically Amazon Web Services (AWS). You'd probably be surprised to learn that AWS has a customer commitment that's hard to beat: When it identifies cost savings, it proactively passes them along to customers in the form of lowered pricing.

Imagine you get an email from AWS. You open it. You read it. You discover that your bill henceforth is *less*, not more. Holy generosity talk trigger!

The operational side of this word-of-mouth generator is complex, as the AWS product set comprises more than 130 services in more than thirty categories, and prices vary by geographic market. Amazon Web Services' pricing matrix is a bit like a snowflake: never the same for any one customer.

But yet it still refuses to engage in even the smallest gesture to make these price decreases notable and talkable. Instead of simply saying "Congrats! We're going to charge you less," AWS treats it with all the fanfare of Journey launching a tour of fourth-rate casinos. It buries the lede in a lengthy email of bulleted items.

This lack of enthusiasm for its own talk trigger of course rubs off on AWS's customers. This is partially why "price reduction" is not a common theme when you analyze and evaluate customer chatter about Amazon Web Services. Like the world's most laissez-faire dragon, AWS is sitting atop a roomful of talk trigger gold and can't be bothered to mention it with anything more than a whisper.

Secrets are the enemy of word of mouth. Even the famous American burger chain In-N-Out, which is renowned for its "secret" menu, published an entire section of its website describing this secret menu and how to navigate it. This is a "secret" the way that "Mariah Carey lip-synchs on television" is a secret.

Employees Keep It Going

Quiz: What do the customers and employees of Five Guys have in common? Answer: Enthusiasm for the fries.

They're all in on the joke and they get where it's headed. Employees help cultivate a culture of discovery for talk triggers by remaining both enthusiastic about them and trained on how to deliver them. This matters. We emphasized the importance of the following as it pertains to the SEE framework in chapter 17: Existing employees can be your greatest word-of-mouth advocates and source of amplification for talk triggers.

As they evolve over time, talk triggers become part of a company's culture. That's true for every example in this book—The Cheesecake Factory, DoubleTree, Holiday World, Americollect, Lockbusters, FreshBooks. Although scary at the onset, doing things differently becomes a point of pride for employees. They'll talk about their experience in a unique context that reinforces the talk trigger. It lends credibility, and customers notice when something feels authentic.

You might even find that a talk trigger creates a cascade of goodwill outside your customer base. It can show up on a company-reviews-and-jobs site like Glassdoor and benefit your recruiting efforts.

One employee review for The Cheesecake Factory sums it up best. Among the pros of working there?

"Vast menu."

Amplifying a talk trigger is a virtuous cycle that keeps itself going. It keeps the talk trigger in active conversation and keeps it relevant. What happens when a talk trigger begins to suffer from declining returns? We'll look at that in chapter 19.

CHAPTER 19

Create Your Next Talk Trigger

What do you do when you love something so much that you have nothing left to say? Author and CEO Andy Sernovitz describes this as "a chocolate problem."

"We all love chocolate (or most of us, anyway). We appreciate the many varieties of it, the ways it can be manipulated into an amazing mole sauce in one bite and a velvety soft banana blanket in another. Chocolate is amazing, and yet, it's hard to say much about it."

Sernovitz says understanding the chocolate problem is how Google has managed to fend off ongoing enthusiasm issues with its Maps product. In the beginning, Google Maps itself was amazing and far superior to MapQuest or any other map service on offer. We talked about it, and then we didn't. It became commonplace and unremarkable.

But then it did something: Google added real-time traffic. Then we talked about Google Maps again. Eventually, real-time traffic became commonplace and unremarkable.

Satellite images were added. Eventually, this also became worthy of nothing but a shrug.

Street-view images came next, and those created a lot of chatter because they are *super creepy*, right? On rollout, people spent *days* exploring all parts of the world, looking for oddities on street-view images. But now we don't talk about it as much.

Things that are great and amazing sometimes have remarkably short shelf lives. They are the comets of word of mouth. Things are talkable until our parents and grandparents begin talking about them, and then nobody finds them remarkable anymore. This is probably the story that the members of Men At Work tell themselves at band reunions.

It's this way not just with Australian pop bands but also with talk triggers. Some of them suffer from short shelf lives. As you raise the bar and deliver something remarkable, over time, that thing can become . . . unremarkable.

Some brands can endure with a talk trigger for many years. DoubleTree has done it with the cookies, but even DoubleTree finds it necessary to reengage and remind customers of the talk trigger, as we outlined in chapter 18 about amplification. The brand knows it needs to reignite the cookie passion, or the trigger itself can become nothing but wallpaper, with chocolate chips.

What are you going to do when the amazing thing that you've championed, loved, coddled, and launched into popularity begins to fade?

Enterprise Rent-A-Car has this issue. It has a long-standing talk trigger whereby it will pick up its customers and/or drop them off back at their home or place of business. For years, every television commercial for the brand used the tagline "We'll Pick You Up!"

At one time this was a strong, talkable differentiator. After all, Avis, Budget, and Alamo vehicle rentals don't pick you up. And if

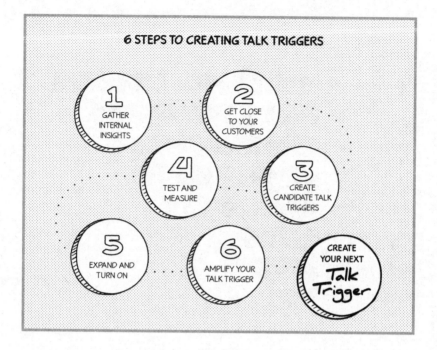

they do, few people know about it or discuss it. Enterprise had a repeatable and relevant talk trigger in the generosity category, and it pressed that advantage for years.

But today it's a talk trigger without the talk. Working with Jason Falls and the Conversational Research Institute, we examined tens of thousands of social media mentions of the Enterprise brand in the fall of 2017, looking for evidence of the power of the "pickup." It's just not there. Within all positive social media mentions of Enterprise, the pickup service was the *eighth* most often mentioned attribute; hardly a dominant word-of-mouth engine.

What happened?

There are three reasons why a successful talk trigger begins to fail, no longer providing the conversational pop it once did.

First, competitors mimic you. Westin Hotels began the "comfy bed in the hotel" craze with its Heavenly Bed, but it couldn't maintain the uniqueness of the differentiator. Hilton Garden Inn,

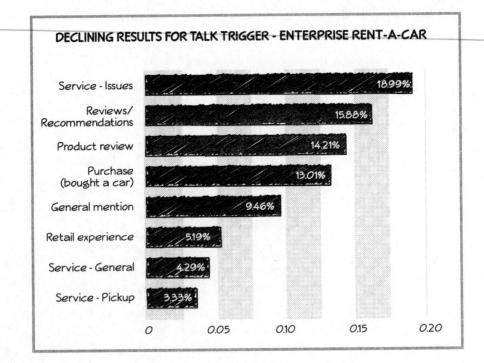

DECLINING RESULTS FOR TALK TRIGGER - ENTERPRISE RENT-A-CAR

Service - Issues	18.99%
Reviews/Recommendations	15.88%
Product review	14.21%
Purchase (bought a car)	13.01%
General mention	9.46%
Retail experience	5.19%
Service - General	4.29%
Service - Pickup	3.33%

0   0.05   0.10   0.15   0.20

Marriott International, and other brands upped their sleep game, making the Heavenly Bed less worthy of conversation.

Second, the talk trigger becomes so well known that it becomes expected, no longer surprising the customer enough to spur chatter. This may be the case with Zappos, which essentially pioneered the concept of free two-way shipping. We suspect nearly 100 percent of Zappos customers now know about and expect that feature, rendering it conversationally inert.

Third, technology and societal norms change, making the talk trigger less interesting and relevant. This might be the case for Enterprise, as the emergence of ridesharing apps Uber and Lyft in the United States has made getting "picked up" for a ride a one-click experience.

Paragon Direct, the automotive company we profiled in chapter 11, picks up vehicles at any time, works on them overnight, and returns them to the customer before he or she leaves for work in the morning. With a speed-based talk trigger like that, it's no wonder that "We'll Pick You Up!" may no longer spur conversations like it once did.

Enterprise appears to recognize the slippage in its talk trigger and often now calls itself a "global transportation solution." The pickup service is still offered, of course, but its details have been relegated to a FAQ item and includes terms and conditions that don't quite leave you feeling warm and fuzzy.

So what do you do when your talk trigger isn't remarkable any longer? Wind it down and create a new one.

Carve a New Path

It's important that you encourage your talk trigger to either evolve or eventually be replaced.

Do you need to fully start over?

Not necessarily. If you're finding that a talk trigger is performing worse over time, you will want to go back through parts of the process we've outlined in this book and reexamine data, insights, and ideas before testing new concepts.

Begin with the elements we outlined in chapter 13 ("Gather Internal Insights") and form a new team, or reassemble your existing team, and bring fresh data to the table. That might not need to be a full-on stand-alone session as it was in the beginning, as you'll have established some working processes for managing talk triggers already. You might have even noticed a cultural shift in your company that makes this step almost unnecessary. We find some organizations behave more reflexively to customer insights than others.

Then follow the processes outlined in chapters 14 ("Get Close to Your Customers") and 15 ("Create Candidate Talk Triggers"). This modified method will generate new ideas that you can map on the

Complexity Map and also gives you fresh, new perspective to use as a group in your Triangle of Awesome.

It's like a Guns N' Roses reunion tour without the long hair or makeup. Same music; updated show.

If you need help with creating new ideas, go back to the five types of talk triggers, the middle of our 4-5-6 system: talkable empathy, talkable usefulness, talkable generosity, talkable speed, and talkable attitude.

And it's always helpful to remind yourself and the group about what a talk trigger really is: a strategic, operational differentiator. It has to be remarkable, repeatable, reasonable, and relevant. Do your new ideas measure up to that metric? If so, plot them on a brand-new Complexity Map.

What kind of ideas are you looking for in the evolution of an existing talk trigger? It's helpful to look at the obvious. You might find that you need to move further down the complexity variable to create something that's related to your existing talk trigger but is truly more unique to your business.

You could also find that cultural or behavioral trends have shifted, making your existing talk trigger execution irrelevant while the underlying premise is still sound. If the way in which your customer consumes the product has changed, your talk trigger may need to change too.

It is worth noting that evolving a talk trigger has its risks. Sometimes companies make changes to a beloved component of their customer experience—one that might not have even been acknowledged as a talk trigger. This was the case for L.L. Bean, which, in early 2018, changed a long-standing return policy that truly did set the company apart. Before the change, its return policy was simple, devoid of terms and conditions: A customer could return a product, for any reason, at any time.

L.L. Bean's generosity was apparently tested by a small percentage of customers who returned items that were decades old for a refund. The new policy is still generous by many standards: A customer can return an item for any reason within one year of purchase. But what the company learned was that by replacing an old return policy that truly was a differentiator with a new, more standard return policy, it invited criticism and damaged its brand in the process. The issue isn't L.L. Bean's new policy. The real issue was its rollout of the change. If you decide to shelve or change a talk trigger, pay attention to how you communicate it to customers.

Add a Talk Trigger

Another approach you may want to explore doesn't involve killing your talk trigger. It involves adding another one, a sibling, to create an entirely new style of conversation.

We look again to Holiday World for a great example of how this works. Remember our first case study about Holiday World: unlimited free beverages. That perk, to this day, is the thing most people mention and talk about, but on its own it becomes a one-act play. It's repeatable, is certainly remarkable and reasonable, and on a hot day it's overwhelmingly relevant.

What if Holiday World created a more quirky sibling to unlimited free drinks? It did it by challenging its team.

Paula Werne, director of communications, says they began with these questions: What's the next big thing? What else can we do besides free soft drinks?

"A couple months later we came back to the table, and the woman who was in charge of the water park at that time had come up with the idea of sunscreen, because who [else] but someone working in a water park every day sees more people not having sunscreen and not using it?"

Sunscreen.

Holiday World jumped on the opportunity and built kiosks to house 55-gallon drums of SPF 30 all around its parks.

"We really promote applying often," said Werne. "Really rub it in, wait a little bit until you get in the water, and then when you get out of the water, go put some more on. It's really promoting people being healthier."

It might seem logical to fear theft of large quantities of sunscreen, creating a massive line-item expense without much upside. To the contrary, the team at Holiday World has found that its guests are very appreciative for the availability of both the sunscreen and free beverages and don't frequently treat it like a trip to Costco or Sam's Club.

"For the most part, people are very appreciative. It's kind of like we work so hard at keeping the park clean, people appreciate that, and they tend to not junk up the park because they see that we keep it clean and they try to do the same thing," said Werne. "It's really looking at it psychologically. It's neat to see when you do something nice for them, they want to do something nice back."

Holiday World has found that its guests give back by not only treating the park and its free soda and gallons of sunscreen with respect, they also frequently share those positive experiences with friends and family and on ratings and reviews sites. This has made its talk triggers—now a suite of brand promises that differentiate its parks from those located literally anywhere else in the United States—a durable and enduring element of the organization's word of mouth.

Commoditization Is Likely (Although Not Inevitable)

As we mentioned in chapter 1, customers hold a lot of the power to build and sustain brands. Commoditization is happening not just in products and services but also in actual brand experiences and promises. Dixon, Toman, and DeLisi write in *The Effortless Experience* that "commoditization . . . is one of the unavoidable hard truths of doing business in the twenty-first century. The time from launch to peak of market acceptance to everyone else ripping off your great new idea and calling it their own is shrinking down to almost nothing. As soon as you think you have something that sets your brand apart, competitors launch an identical product or service or claim."

According to our research, customers view only 20 percent of businesses as "truly differentiated." In truth, most customers don't find things remarkable because they just aren't different enough. What makes a particular idea or thing talkable changes over time, and your talk trigger may need to eventually change as well.

Same Is Lame

Being exceedingly competent at whatever it is you do isn't enough. Operational excellence and strong customer experience helps you to keep the customers you've already earned; and that's a worthy objective unto itself. But *good* is a four-letter word. It doesn't catalyze much conversation because consumers increasingly expect and anticipate businesses to deliver high-level customer experiences.

You need more than that. You need a talk trigger to give your customers the needed ingredients to tell your story persuasively, and with impact.

You now know the four criteria for a differentiator to be a talk trigger. You've discovered the five distinct types of talk triggers. You've learned the six-step process for how to create your own word-of-mouth engine.

The rest is up to you.

Same is lame. Give yourself permission to do something different. Something noteworthy. Something talkable.

Don't forget we have many additional resources to help you at TalkTriggers.com. There might even be a little talk trigger there for you to find!

Also, we created a quick reference guide that begins in the appendix. It highlights the important data and key lessons in *Talk Triggers* so you can easily refer back to your word-of-mouth journey.

And finally, a request. If you like this book, please tell your friends. ;)

Jay Baer and Daniel Lemin
2018

APPENDIX:
QUICK REFERENCE GUIDE

If you've just finished reading the book, congratulations.

You're well on your way to creating customer conversations and building your business with talk triggers. We've provided this easy reference guide so that you can quickly refresh your understanding of the key principles when needed. Also, we've noted every case study in the book, the size and industry type of each company, and whether a company is B2B (business to business) or B2C (business to consumer). This may be useful for you if you remember a *Talk Triggers* example some day and want to easily find and reread it.

If you're the kind of person who flips to the back of the book right away, this reference guide will give you an idea of what's included in *Talk Triggers*.

Many more free resources are available to you, including an online community where you can discuss word of mouth with your peers and with us. Go to TalkTriggers.com to begin. And feel free to contact us anytime at JayAndDaniel@TalkTriggers.com.

CHAPTER 1: TALK IS CHEAP

Case Study
- The Cheesecake Factory (large, B2C, restaurant)

Key Points
- Word of mouth is more effective than ever.
- Consumers' trust in one another is increasing as trust in companies decreases.
- Word of mouth works best when the information exchanged is specific.
- A talk trigger is a purposeful, operational differentiator that creates conversation among customers and recruits potential new customers in the process.

Key Data
- Nineteen percent of all consumer purchases in the United States are directly caused by word of mouth.
- In the United States, United Kingdom, Brazil, and China, word of mouth influences purchase decisions more than any other factor.
- The impact of word of mouth on B2B is even greater.

CHAPTER 2: STEER THE CONVERSATION

Case Study
- DoubleTree by Hilton Hotels and Resorts (large, B2C, hospitality)

Key Points
- Offline word of mouth is often more robust because consumers don't curate their experiences the way they do online, on social media.
- Social media does not equal word of mouth. It is one of the conveyances of word of mouth.

- Some word of mouth will always occur, but the best businesses are intentional about causing conversations.

Key Data

- Small businesses say word of mouth is their most effective sales channel.
- Online and offline word of mouth are each about 50 percent of the total conversations about businesses.
- We estimate less than 1 percent of businesses have a specific plan for word-of-mouth marketing.

CHAPTER 3: SAME IS LAME

Case Study

- WindsorONE Lumber (medium, B2B, manufacturing)

Key Points

- A unique selling proposition is a feature. A talk trigger is a benefit, articulated with a story.
- In the context of word-of-mouth generation, being "good" is not enough.
- There are four groups of customers in a word-of-mouth scenario: uniqueness seekers, experience advisors, fundamentals fans, and skeptics.
- Experience advisors are consumers often asked for their opinion by others. Uniqueness seekers explicitly look for companies that are different. Fundamentals fans look for "good" routine experiences. Skeptics say they reject differentiators from businesses.

Key Data

- Recounting a direct experience with a product, service, or company is the most powerful form of conversation and represents as much as 80 percent of all word-of-mouth activity.

CHAPTER 4: BE REMARKABLE

Case Studies
- Umpqua Bank (large, B2C and B2B, financial services)
- Lockbusters (small, B2C, services)

Key Points
- We naturally seek to be better instead of different.
- People rarely discuss perfectly adequate experiences.
- There are four criteria for a differentiator to be a talk trigger: remarkable, relevant, reasonable, and repeatable.

Key Data
- No differentiator will be beloved by 100 percent of customers; if that were the case, it wouldn't be different enough to create conversations.

CHAPTER 5: BE RELEVANT

Case Studies
- Holiday World and Splashin' Safari (medium, B2C, and hospitality)
- FreshBooks (medium, B2B, software)

Key Points
- Your talk trigger should support your company's overall positioning and tone.
- Events can be a terrific complement to talk triggers.

CHAPTER 6: BE REASONABLE

Case Studies
- Graduate Hotels (small, B2C, hospitality)
- Five Guys Enterprises (large, B2C, restaurant)

Key Points

- Customers are suspicious when businesses offer something that seems too good to be true, because it often is.
- Your differentiator needs to be bold enough to create conversation but reasonable enough to be believed.
- Talk triggers have to be simple enough to explain in one sentence.

Key Data

- When you overpromise consumers, it not only reduces participation but also diminishes brand trust in the future.

CHAPTER 7: BE REPEATABLE

Case Studies

- Penn & Teller (medium, B2C, entertainment)
- Clube de Jornalistas (small business, B2C, restaurant)

Key Points

- Surprise and delight is a publicity stunt, not a word-of-mouth strategy.
- Talk triggers are not marketing (like a campaign or a promotion) but rather consistently applied operational differentiators that create marketing advantages.
- Consistency trumps delight and builds trust.
- Inconsistent customer treatment breeds confusion and distrust.

CHAPTER 8: TALKABLE EMPATHY

Case Studies

- Americollect (medium, B2B, financial services)
- Dr. Glenn Gorab (small business, B2C, health care)

Key Points

- There are five types of talk triggers: empathy, usefulness, generosity, speed, and attitude.
- Empathy and humanity are effective talk triggers because most businesses operate with only small doses (if any) of either.

Key Data

- Physicians who are more empathetic are sued less often by their patients.

CHAPTER 9: TALKABLE USEFULNESS

Case Studies

- Air New Zealand (large, B2C and B2B, transportation)
- Spiceworks (medium, B2B, software)

Key Point

- For companies that do not have the emotional scaffolding to use empathy as a talk trigger, consider usefulness: giving customers more utility than they anticipate.

CHAPTER 10: TALKABLE GENEROSITY

Case Studies

- Flanders Meeting & Convention Center Antwerp (medium, B2B, hospitality)
- Skip's Kitchen (small, B2C, restaurant)

Key Point

- Many businesses are trying to boost profit margins by giving consumers less. Generosity talk triggers work because they give consumers much more than they expect.

Key Data

- Shrinkflation—when portion sizes get smaller but prices remain the same—is more and more common, making generosity talk triggers even more noticeable.
- A restaurant's physical environment is the most important factor in influencing dining choices.

CHAPTER 11: TALKABLE SPEED

Case Studies

- Paragon Direct (medium, B2C, automotive)
- KLM Royal Dutch Airlines (large, B2C, B2B, transportation)

Key Points

- Nothing ever gets slower.
- What was considered responsive three years ago is table stakes (at best) today.
- To be talkably swift is a high standard.

Key Data

- Forty-one percent of consumers say that when they contact a business, "getting my issue resolved quickly" is the most important element of a good customer experience.
- Speed is rated 350 percent more important than "politeness of the company representative."
- More than nine in ten Americans say they refuse to wait on hold for more than five minutes when telephoning a business.

CHAPTER 12: TALKABLE ATTITUDE

Case Studies
- EC Chantal (small, B2C, services/manufacturing)
- Uberflip (small, B2B, software)
- UberConference (medium, B2B, telecommunications)

Key Points
- Most businesses are manifestly serious, so choosing to take a different approach can create an effective talk trigger.
- To work, an attitude talk trigger has to be embraced at all levels of the company, including (and perhaps in particular) the executive level.

CHAPTER 13: GATHER INTERNAL INSIGHTS

Key Points
- There are six steps to follow when creating your own talk trigger: Gather internal insights, get close to your customers, create candidate talk triggers, test and measure, expand and turn on, and amplify your talk trigger.
- Talk triggers aren't "owned" by any department; they cut across the entire company.
- Your Triangle of Awesome is a group of team members from marketing, sales, and service who come together to work on talk triggers.
- In step one, your participating team members gather existing data about your customers, your business, and your competitors.

CHAPTER 14: GET CLOSE TO YOUR CUSTOMERS

Key Points

- Many people in business aren't certain what customers want or need because they spend very little time around customers.
- Research and surveys can show you at a surface level what customers want, but rarely what they *really* want.
- Social media conversation data can help illuminate customers' true feelings.
- Product or service usage data show not just what customers say they want but also what they are actually doing today.
- Conversations with sales and service people in your business can help to illuminate customer wants.
- Experiencing your business firsthand, just as a customer would, can help you identify potential talk triggers.

CHAPTER 15: CREATE CANDIDATE TALK TRIGGERS

Key Points

- Remembering the four criteria of a talk trigger and the five types of talk triggers, find four to six potential ideas for your business that give customers what they *really* want.
- There are two levels of talk trigger: product and brand. It's usually best to begin with product level.
- Plot your potential talk triggers on a Complexity Map that looks at low, medium, and high complexity versus low, medium, and high impact.
- The ideal spot on a Complexity Map for a first talk trigger is at medium impact and medium complexity.
- Understand in advance what potential obstacles and objections will mean, regarding the talk triggers in your business, so that you can solve them quickly.

CHAPTER 16: TEST AND MEASURE YOUR TALK TRIGGERS

Key Points

- The impact of talk triggers on word of mouth—and overall business success—is possible to measure; it just may take a while and require some manual work.
- The effectiveness of talk triggers may be partially evident when viewing your customers' social media conversations, email, reviews, and the like.
- Offline word of mouth is incredibly powerful and it may require surveying your customers to find and to isolate its impact.
- Before you take your candidate talk trigger full scale, test it with a subset of your customers. You are looking for a 10 percent or greater conversation rate (one in ten customers mentions the talk trigger—unaided—when asked about what is different about your business).

CHAPTER 17: EXPAND AND TURN ON

Key Points

- If your candidate talk trigger is exceeding a 10 percent conversation rate in a test environment, consider rolling it out to the entire company.
- Once taken full scale and amplified, your talk trigger should yield a 25 percent conversation rate to be viable for the long term.
- Three key groups in your company need to be supportive of your word-of-mouth efforts for them to be effective and sustainable: stakeholders, employees, and the business at large.
- When taking a talk trigger full scale, having an executive to champion the cause inside the organization can be of great benefit.

- Merchandise the success of the talk trigger organizationwide: If employees don't know or care about your differentiator, why will customers?

CHAPTER 18: AMPLIFY YOUR TALK TRIGGER

Key Points

- Once you have the beginnings of a successful talk trigger, help it take root and flourish by making it known to customers.
- Create your "because" statement to help explain why the talk trigger exists and for whom it's intended.
- Some of the best talk triggers are amplified in their company's paid advertising.

Key Data

- Word of mouth drives five times more sales than advertising.

CHAPTER 19: CREATE YOUR NEXT TALK TRIGGER

Key Points

- Some talk triggers can succeed for years, even decades. But others cease to create conversation when customer expectations shift.
- When you see your talk trigger's conversation rate declining, or notice that competitors are mimicking what was once unique to you, go back to the beginning of the six-step process to find a new differentiator.
- Instead of a wholly new trigger, you may be able to add to or elevate an existing one.

- Talk triggers turn your current customers into volunteer marketers.

Key Data

- Somewhere between two and five of every ten dollars your company earns is because of word of mouth.

ACKNOWLEDGMENTS

A work like *Talk Triggers* is truly a team effort. First, a huge thank-you to my brilliant collaborator and friend, Daniel Lemin. He is a terrific author and a world-class human being. It's an honor to bring this project to life with him.

I cannot describe here the love and appreciation I have for my family. This is the sixth book I have written or cowritten, and each time my wife, Alyson, daughter, Annika, and son, Ethan, make myriad sacrifices and accommodations so that I can stay in "book mode" long enough to come out the other end with something that benefits readers. Thank you.

Thanks also to my amazing team at Convince & Convert, where we work with many of the world's most iconic brands to help them create talk triggers and improve their marketing and customer service. I am truly blessed to be surrounded every day with professionals of their caliber.

Special recognition to Kristina Paider, who handled first-draft editing and overall shaping of the manuscript in the early stages of this creation.

We are also indebted to Susan Baier at Audience Audit for her excellent work on the custom consumer attitudinal research we conducted for this book. Thank you, Susan.

Thank you also to our literary agent, Jim Levine, whose guidance and insights are simply incalculable in their value.

An emphatic round of high fives to the entire team at Penguin Portfolio, most especially our very supportive editor, Merry Sun.

And, of course, this book simply would not exist without the incredible contributions of the many companies, researchers, academics, authors, and consultants who graciously lent their time and insights for inclusion in *Talk Triggers*. They include (in order of appearance): Ted Wright (thank you for your foreword), John Jantsch, Jonah Berger, Ed Keller, Andy Sernovitz, Stuart Foster, Scott McKain, Sally Hogshead, Emanuel Rosen, Brian Bunt, Craig Flynn, Jay Sofer, Paula Werne, Matt Eckert, Mike McDerment, Spike Jones, Luisa Torres Branco, Kenlyn Gretz, Deanna Christesen, Dr. Glenn Gorab, Jay Hallberg, Anja Stas, Skip Wahl, Brian Benstock, Kaleb Ryan, Randy Frisch, Sean Ellis, and Jackie Woodward.

—Jay Baer

This book was a true delight to outline, write, research, and edit. The stories are filled with gorgeous details and lots of humanity, and we had the chance to become acquainted with some truly great people along the way (Jay Sofer at Lockbusters, Mike McDerment at Freshbooks—you guys rock).

Somewhere in our respective phone archives is a selfie of me and Jay Baer. It was taken at Jay's lake house in the middle of December, where we clambered down onto the boat dock and risked falling into nearly frozen water to get just the right shot.

If I look frozen in this picture, it's because I was truly . . . frozen in this picture. It was such a privilege and joy to collaborate with Jay on this book. His enthusiasm and energy are boundless, and I'm grateful for the many years we've had working together.

A big project like a book requires an army of people to make it work. It takes grit and gratitude. I'm grateful for the time given generously to us by so many people, noted by Jay above.

Grateful for Steven, who patiently kept the lights on and helped me stay fed and watered during the months of writing and research.

Grateful for my friends Lisa Loeffler and Aram Malinich, who were present for much of the writing and served as a sounding board so many times over a martini.

Grateful for Merry Sun at Penguin Portfolio. Jay's right on the money: She was supportive, enthusiastic, and is an excellent editing partner.

Grateful for Chris Anthony Torregosa, who is responsible for all of the delightful little illustrations you see throughout this book.

Grateful for Alex Cornell, who wrote the great hold music as cofounder of UberConference. If you've seen me give a talk about this book live you know how much I love that music. I still get a kick out of my time on hold!

A book is never *really* finished, and I'm looking forward to seeing how our community of readers puts these tools to use.

—Daniel Lemin

AUTHORS' NOTE

This book is all about the power of people. Your voice—offline and online—determines almost entirely whether *Talk Triggers* is successful in its quest to help businesses of all sizes be more strategic and effective in the creation of customer conversation.

So, if you like *Talk Triggers*, please talk about it! And if you do so online, tag us and/or use the hashtag #TalkTriggers. We'll be handing out special awards for noteworthy talkable moments.

Also, remember that there are many additional resources about talk triggers and how to create them that didn't fit in the book. Go to TalkTriggers.com to access videos, webinars, new case studies, worksheets, and special surprises.

WE BUILD TALK TRIGGERS
We also work directly with companies to help them identify, plan, test, measure, and operationalize winning talk trigger

differentiators. If you're intrigued by the premise of talk triggers but would like some help making it work in your organization, send us a note at JayAndDaniel@TalkTriggers.com and we'll be in touch immediately.

TALK TRIGGERS ON STAGE

We also travel the world spreading the message of talk triggers and the importance of word of mouth. We'd be honored to collaborate with you on a keynote, customized workshop, webinar, or other live training opportunity. Just email us at the address above.

NOTES

Chapter 1: Talk Is Cheap

3   **85 different chicken dishes:** Danya Henninger, "The Cheesecake Factory Is About to Open: We Broke Down the Menu," *Billy Penn*, last modified June 7, 2015, https://billypenn.com/2015/06/07/the -cheesecake-factory-is-about-to-open-we-broke-down-the-menu/.

4   **Twitter alone produced:** Figure 1: Christopher (@potterhead0499), "I've been to Cheesecake Factory a hundred times," Twitter, November 19, 2017, 4:56 a.m., https://twitter.com/potterhead0499/status /932185839886532608; Figure 2: Austin (@TheRisky_Ginger), "The Cheesecake Factory menu is like a very weird book," Twitter, November 17, 2017, 2:25 p.m., https://twitter.com/TheRisky_Ginger/status /931604330041393152; Figure 3: Greg Mania (@Greg Mania), "What book do you want to see made into a movie?" Twitter, November 17, 2017, 7:26 p.m., https://twitter.com/gregmania/status /931680096049606656.

4   **customers refer to it:** Figure 4: CECE (@cece24_lovesu), "My mom just said 'we should go to the gigantic menu,'" Twitter, November 5,

2017, 4:12 p.m., https://twitter.com/cece24_lovesu/status /927282511771713537.

5   **total sales on advertising:** Ralph Nathan, "What Is The Cheesecake Factory's Marketing Strategy?" Market Realist, last modified June 2, 2016, https://marketrealist.com/2016/06/cheesecake-factorys -marketing-strategy.

5   **advertising (as a percentage of sales):** Ibid.

5   **increase in restaurant sales:** David Godes and Dina Mayzlin, "Firm-Created Word-of-Mouth Communication: Evidence from a Field Test," *Marketing Science* 28, no. 4 (July–August 2009): 721–39, https:// msbfile03.usc.edu/digitalmeasures/mayzlin/intellcont/godes_mayzlin _09-1.pdf.

7   **"first-ever product of its kind":** Definition for "Unique Selling Point (USP)," WhatIS.com, last accessed March 11, 2018, http://whatis .techtarget.com/definition/unique-selling-point-USP.

9   **word-of-mouth activity:** "New Study Finds that 19 Percent of Sales Are Driven by Consumer Conversations Taking Place Offline and Online," Engagement Labs, last modified November 27, 2017, www .engagementlabs.com/press/new-study-finds-19-percent-sales-driven -consumer-conversations-taking-place-offline-online/.

9   **number of total customers:** "New Study Shows What Influences B2B Tech Purchase Decisions," Business Wire, last modified October 14, 2015, www.businesswire.com/news/home/20151014006145/en/New -Study-Shows-Influences-B2B-Tech-Purchase.

9   **for these three reasons:** Jillian C. Sweeney, Geoffrey N. Soutar, and Time Mazzarol, eds., "The Differences between Positive and Negative Word-of-Mouth—Emotion as a Differentiator?" (report, ANZMAC Conference: Consumer Behaviour, Perth, Australia, 2005): 331–37, https://cemi.com.au/sites/all/publications/3-Sweeney.pdf.

9   **increasingly desire personalization:** "Customers Welcome Personalized Offerings but Businesses Are Struggling to Deliver, Finds Accenture Interactive Personalization Research," Accenture Newsroom, last modified October 13, 2016, https://newsroom.accenture.com/news /consumers-welcome-personalized-offerings-but-businesses-are -struggling-to-deliver-finds-accenture-interactive-personalization -research.htm.

10 **asynchronous word of mouth:** "Recommendations from Friends Remain Most Credible Form of Advertising among Consumers; Branded

Websites Are the Second-Highest Rated Form," Nielsen Press Room, last modified September 28, 2015, www.nielsen.com/us/en/press-room /2015/recommendations-from-friends-remain-most-credible-form -of-advertising.html.

10   **they trust companies:** Edelman, *2018 Edelman Trust Barometer,* Global Report (New York and Chicago: Edelman, 2018), 38, http://cms .edelman.com/sites/default/files/2018-02/2018_Edelman_Trust _Barometer_Global_Report_FEB.pdf.

10   **revenue came from referrals:** John Jantsch, *The Referral Engine: Teaching Your Business to Market Itself* (New York: Portfolio, 2012), 11.

10   **"most referrals happen by accident":** John Jantsch, telephone interview with Jay Baer, November 3, 2017.

Chapter 2: Steer the Conversation

13   **marketers and business owners:** Jonah Berger, telephone interview with Jay Baer, November 6, 2017.

14   **in different circumstances:** Engagement Labs, "Word of mouth still rules," December 1, 2017, https://www.engagementlabs.com/news /word-mouth-still-rules-consumer-conversations-drive-sales/.

14   **"desire for social signaling":** This quote and next from Ed Keller, telephone interview with Jay Baer, November 9, 2017.

15   **research from the Keller Fay Group:** Ed Keller and Brad Fay, "Word-of-Mouth Advocacy: A New Key to Advertising Effectiveness," *Journal of Advertising Research 52,* no. 4 (December 1, 2012): 460, https://doi.org/10.2501/JAR-52-4-459-464.

15   **When booking a vacation:** Marios D. Sotiriadis and Cinà van Zyl, "Electronic Word-of-Mouth and Online Reviews in Tourism Services: The Use of Twitter by Tourists," *Electronic Commerce Research* 13, no. 1 (March 2013):103–24, https://doi.org/10.1007/s10660-013-9108-1.

15   **40,369 other potential customers:** Ted Wright, telephone interview with Jay Baer, November 4, 2017.

15   **networks we most value:** Jacques Bughin, Jonathan Doogan, and Ole Jørgen Vetvik, "A New Way to Measure Word-of-Mouth Marketing," McKinsey Quarterly, McKinsey & Company, last modified April 2010, www.mckinsey.com/business-functions/marketing-and-sales/our -insights/a-new-way-to-measure-word-of-mouth-marketing.

16   **$23.6 billion in 2019:** BIA/Kelsey, "Social Media Advertising Spending in the United States from 2012 to 2019, by Type (in billion U.S. dollars)"

Statista, last accessed December 1, 2017, www.statista.com/statistics
/246339/social-media-advertising-spending-in-the-us-by-type/.

16   **"it's just a tool":** Andy Sernovitz, telephone interview with Jay Baer,
November 7, 2017.

18   **in each hotel:** Stuart Foster, telephone interview with Jay Baer, October
17, 2017.

19   **"this cult following":** Ibid.

21   **nearly seven hundred retweets:** Figure 8: DoubleTree by Hilton
(@doubletree), "In this hotel we give," Twitter, November 10, 2017, 9:58
a.m., https://twitter.com/doubletree/status/929000364795486208.

21   **cookie with this tweet:** Figure 9: Becka Hawkins Beatty (@Rebelesq1)
"Marriage is basically trusting your spouse," Twitter, November 23,
2017, 9:59 p.m., https://twitter.com/Rebelesq1/status
/933892760498851846.

Chapter 3: Same Is Lame

24   **"acts like Alice Cooper":** Alan Light, "'Ziggy Stardust': How Bowie
Created the Alter Ego that Changed Rock," *Rolling Stone*, last modified
June 16, 2016, www.rollingstone.com/music/features/ziggy-stardust
-how-bowie-created-the-alter-ego-that-changed-rock-20160616.

25   **"sustained growth and profitability":** Scott McKain, *Create
Distinction: What to Do When "Great" Isn't Good Enough to Grow*
(Austin: Greenleaf Book Group, 2013), 44–45.

25   **as a competitive advantage:** Michele McGovern, "Customers Want
More: 5 New Expectations You Must Meet Now," Customer Experience
Insight, last modified June 30, 2016, www.customerexperienceinsight
.com/customer-expectations-you-must-meet-now/.

26   **"the product or service itself":** Emanuel Rosen, *The Anatomy of Buzz
Revisited: Real-Life Lessons in Word-of-Mouth Marketing* (New York:
Crown Business, 2009), 145.

27   **"lower relative to them":** Sally Hogshead, telephone interview with Jay
Baer, November 7, 2017.

28   **"came up with some ideas":** Brian Bunt and Craig Flynn, telephone
interview with Jay Baer, November 2, 2017.

30   **"Short, sharable stories rule":** Robbin Phillips, Greg Cordell, Geno
Church, and John Moore, *The Passion Conversation: Understanding,
Sparking, and Sustaining Word of Mouth Marketing* (Hoboken, NJ:
John Wiley & Sons, 2013), 50.

Chapter 4: Be Remarkable

42   "the same direction": Youngme Moon, *Different: Escaping the Competitive Herd* (New York: Crown Business, 2010), loc. 2174 of 288, Kindle.

45   fifty largest banking chains: Kurt Badenhausen, "Full List: Ranking America's 100 Largest Banks 2018," *Forbes*, last updated January 10, 2018, https://www.forbes.com/sites/kurtbadenhausen/2018/01/10 /full-list-ranking-americas-100-largest-banks-2018/.

45   in a 2013 article: Jeffry Pilcher, "New Umpqua Flagship Store Shatters Stuffy Branch Mold," The Financial Brand, last updated August 26, 2013, https://thefinancialbrand.com/33026/umpqua-bank-san -francisco-flagship-branch/.

45   valuable the hotline is: Figure 19: Umpqua Bank (@umpqua), "What makes us unique?" Twitter, June 22, 2009, 1:37 p.m., https://twitter .com/umpquabank/status/2281853722; Figure 20: Adrian Simpson (@AdieSimpson), "At #Umpqua Bank any customer can," Twitter, September 28, 2017, 1:13 a.m., https://twitter.com/AdieSimpson/status /913270321209384965.

46   "answer those questions": Julia La Roche, "Umpqua Bank Offers Customers Direct Access to Its CEO from Its Stores," *Business Insider*, last modified February 28, 2012, www.businessinsider.com/umpqua -bank-offers-customers-direct-access-to-its-ceo-from-its-stores-2012-2? op=1.

47   authentic or a gimmick: "Umpqua Bank Branching Out: An Odd Bank from an Odd City Is Doing Oddly Well," *Economist*, last updated June 12, 2014, www.economist.com/news/finance-and-economics/ 21604218-odd-bank-odd-city-doing-oddly-well-branching-out.

47   all of New York City: Lockbusters: "Jay The Locksmith," posted by Yelp Studios, uploaded on November 16, 2011, featuring award for Jay Sofer announced by former New York City mayor Michael Bloomberg, video, 3:37, www.youtube.com/watch?v=T90Na6opT4k.

47   system . . . of penetrability: "Secure Your Home," Lockbusters, last accessed February 25, 2018, www.lockbustersnyc.com/secure-your -home/.

48   Sofer on his website: "About Lockbusters," Lockbusters, last accessed February 25, 2018, www.lockbustersnyc.com/about-lockbusters/.

49   Sofer told us: Jay Sofer, telephone interview with Daniel Lemin, December 1, 2017.

49   **"experience was that great":** Chantelle D., "Is it weird I almost want
to get locked out again," Yelp, January 24, 2010, www.yelp.com/biz
/lockbusters-new-york?hrid=_cmwaawbGQbLV44EEN2cDw.

50   **Sheila M.:** Figure 22: Sheila M., "After the worst ever locksmith
experience," Yelp, March 28, 2017, www.yelp.com/biz/lockbusters-new
-york?hrid=Qo0gLTaNTSlCTrIOiCxWcw.

Chapter 5: Be Relevant

54   **"What can we do differently":** All quotes in the discussion about
Holiday World from Paula Werne and Matt Eckert, telephone interview
with Jay Baer, November 2, 2017.

56   **explicitly mention free drinks:** "Holiday Word & Splashin' Safari,"
Review Highlights, TripAdvisor, last accessed February 25, 2018, www
.tripadvisor.com/Attraction_Review-g37506-d126379-Reviews
-Holiday_World_Splashin_Safari-Santa_Claus_Indiana.html; Figure
24: DaleS820, "Great Value," TripAdvisor, October 2, 2017, www
.tripadvisor.com/ShowUserReviews-g37506-d126379-r529241675
-Holiday_World_Splashin_Safari-Santa_Claus_Indiana
.html#review529241675; Figure 25: G1989DRhollyp, "Lots of family
fun!" TripAdvisor, August 23, 2017, www.tripadvisor.com
/ShowUserReviews-g37506-d126379-r516791213-Holiday_World
_Splashin_Safari-Santa_Claus_Indiana.html#review516791213; Figure
26: darlable, "Fun times," TripAdvisor, July 26, 2017, www.tripadvisor
.com/ShowUserReviews-g37506-d126379-r505964717-Holiday_World
_Splashin_Safari-Santa_Claus_Indiana.html#review505964717.

57   **house in Toronto:** Mike McDerment, telephone interview with Daniel
Lemin, December 2, 2017.

58   **Attendees clearly value it:** Figure 27: Kasumi (@kasumisohh), "At the
#IMakeaLiving event powered by @freshbooks," Twitter, November
29, 2017, 10:54 a.m., https://twitter.com/kasumisohh/status
/935899682374602754.

Chapter 6: Be Reasonable

61   **daytime talk show:** Kelly Philips Erb, "A Look Back at Oprah's
Ultimate Car Giveaway," *Forbes*, last modified September 13, 2016,
www.forbes.com/sites/kellyphillipserb/2016/09/13/a-look
-back-at-oprahs-ultimate-car-giveaway/#4f5990e560ff.

61   **ranked by Oprah herself:** "15 of the *Oprah Show*'s Greatest
     Giveaways: Everyone Gets a Car!" Oprah, last accessed April 2, 2018,
     www.oprah.com/oprahshow/top-oprah-show-giveaways/all.

62   **taxes on their "free" Pontiacs:** "Oprah Car Winners Hit with Hefty
     Tax," CNN Money, last updated September 22, 2004, http://money.cnn
     .com/2004/09/22/news/newsmakers/oprah_car_tax/.

62   **trust into the future:** Peter R. Darke and Robin J. B. Ritchie, "The
     Defensive Consumer: Advertising Deception, Defensive Processing, and
     Distrust," *Journal of Marketing Research* 44, no. 1 (February, 2007):
     114–27, www.jstor.org/stable/30162458.

64   **award on the brand:** Margaret Rhodes, "This College-Town Hotel
     Chain Is Putting Airbnb on Notice," *Inc.*, last modified May 15, 2017,
     www.inc.com/magazine/201706/margaret-rhodes/graduate-hotels
     -design-awards-2017.html.

64   **Weprin, company founder:** David Hochman, "Inspired by Indiana
     Jones, Graduate Hotels Remakes a Berkeley Landmark," *Forbes*, last
     modified April 25, 2017, https://forbes.com/sites/davidhochman/2017
     /04/25/inspired-by-indiana-jones-graduate-hotels-remakes-a-berkeley
     -landmark/#7ac74c751877.

66   **keys last year:** SI Vault (@si_vault), "The room keys at the Graduate
     Hotel," Twitter, June 24, 2017, 12:02 p.m., twitter.com/si_vault/status
     /878644501040046080.

66   **Cooper Manning:** Jay Bilas (@JayBilas), "Just checked into The
     Graduate in Oxford, MS," Twitter, December 28, 2016, 1:21 p.m.,
     https://twitter.com/JayBilas/status/814174458915287042.

66   **owns the hotel:** "Current Portfolio," AJ Capital Partners, last accessed
     February 25, 2018, http://ajcpt.com/.

67   **"or go to college":** "The Five Guys Story," Five Guys, last accessed
     February 25, 2018, www.fiveguys.com/Fans/The-Five-Guys-Story.

67   **fastest-growing restaurant brand:** Monte Burke, "Five Guys Burgers:
     America's Fastest Growing Restaurant Chain," *Forbes*, last modified
     July 18, 2012, www.forbes.com/forbes/2012/0806/restaurant
     -chefs-12-five-guys-jerry-murrell-all-in-the-family.html#2fe55cb34ee4.

67   **an equal number in development:** Ibid.

68   **"you can't make fries like ours":** Chris Chamberlain, "How the Five
     Guys French Fries Get Made: A Food Republic Exclusive!" Food
     Republic, last modified March 29, 2016, www.foodrepublic.com/2016
     /03/29/how-the-five-guys-french-fries-get-made-a-food-republic
     -exclusive/.

69   **show up on Twitter:** Figure 31: Ryan Yoxtheimer (@yoxryan), "The
~~struggle of getting my burger out,"~~ Twitter, November 21, 2017, 3:21
p.m., https://twitter.com/yoxryan/status/933067772732628993.

69   **french fries, top and bottom:** Figure 32: Christina M
(@ChristinaMets15), "The best part about @Five_Guys is that they,"
Twitter, November 24, 2017, 10:25 a.m., https://twitter.com
/ChristinaMets15/status/934080459566436352; Figure 33: Laura
(@laura_allison99), "The amount of extra fries you always find,"
Twitter, November 18, 2017, 3:38 p.m., https://twitter.com/laura
_allison99/status/931984998256738304.

70   **"get their money's worth":** Chamberlain, "Five Guys French Fries Get
Made."

70   **"giving them enough fries":** Ibid.

70   **"no good reason for it":** Seth Godin, *Purple Cow: Transform Your
Business by Being Remarkable*, New Edition (New York: Portfolio,
2009), 163.

Chapter 7: Be Repeatable

72   **at the airport:** Peter Shankman, "The Greatest Customer Service Story
Ever Told, Starring Morton's Steakhouse," *Peter Shankman* (blog), last
modified August 18, 2011, www.shankman.com/the-greatest-customer
-service-story-ever-told-starring-mortons-steakhouse/.

72   **"will always trump delight":** Jake Sorofman, "In Customer
Experience, Consistency Is the New Delight," *Garter for Marketers*
(blog), last modified July 30, 2015, https://blogs.gartner.com/jake
-sorofman/in-customer-experience-consistency-is-the-new-delight/.

73   **"not just one day, but every day":** Phillips, *The Passion Conversation*, 30.

74   **variety of virtuoso:** "I Want to Hire Magicians in Las Vegas, NV,"
GigSalad, last accessed February 25, 2018, www.gigsalad.com/Magic
/Magician/NV/Las+Vegas.

75   **"pay a hundred bucks":** Jay Jones, "In Often-Pricey Vegas, Magicians
Penn & Teller Continue a Free Tradition," Travel News & Deals, *Los
Angeles Times*, last modified July 13, 2016, www.latimes.com/travel
/deals/la-tr-vegas-penn-teller-free-20160712-snap-story.html.

75   **photographs and merchandise:** D C, "Don't buy the 'Meet and Greet'
ticket," TripAdvisor, August 5, 2016, www.tripadvisor.com
/ShowUserReviews-g45963-d1630313-r401732818-David_Copperfield
-Las_Vegas_Nevada.html.

76   **the post-performance interaction:** Figure 35: Heather_S07, "Great show!" TripAdvisor, May 3, 2016, www.tripadvisor.co.nz/ShowUser Reviews-g45963-d553199-r369857492-Penn_Teller-Las_Vegas_Nevada .html#REVIEWS.

77   **"it was wonderful":** Lesley Nagy, "At the Penn & Teller Show: 7 Questions with Teller," *Huffington Post,* last modified December 6, 2017, https://www.huffingtonpost.com/lesley-nagy/at-the-penn-teller -show-7_b_6117566.html.

77   **"why doesn't everybody":** Nagy, "Penn & Teller Show."

77   **according to TripAdvisor:** "Clube de Jornalistas," Restaurants, TripAdvisor, last accessed February 25, 2018, www.tripadvisor.com /Restaurant_Review-g189158-d945588-Reviews-Clube_de_Jornalistas -Lisbon_Lisbon_District_Central_Portugal.html.

78   **co-owner of the restaurant:** Luisa Torres Branco, email interview with Daniel Lemin, December 15, 2017.

79   **word-of-mouth device:** Figure 36: Joseph S, "First dinner in Lisbon," TripAdvisor, March 12, 2016, www.tripadvisor.com/ShowUserReviews -g189158-d945588-r354821172-Clube_de_Jornalistas-Lisbon_Lisbon _District_Central_Portugal.html#REVIEWS.

Chapter 8: Talkable Empathy

89   **$25 million:** Quotes and information about Americollect from Kenlyn Gretz, telephone interview with Jay Baer, November 6, 2017.

90   **"treat us as a client ridiculously nice":** This quote and the next from Deanna Christesen, telephone interview with Jay Baer, December 4, 2017.

92   **"prior to your appointment":** All quotes this section from Dr. Glenn Gorab, telephone interview with Jay Baer, November 22, 2017.

93   **lawsuit during their career:** Anupam B. Jena, Seth Seabury, Darius Lakdawalla, and Amitabh Chandra, "Malpractice Risk According to Physician Specialty," *New England Journal of Medicine* 365, no. 7 (August 18, 2011): 629–36, www.nejm.org/doi/full/10.1056 /NEJMsa1012370.

Chapter 9: Talkable Usefulness

96   **produced by Air New Zealand:** "9 Best Air New Zealand Safety Videos," Backpacker Guide NV, last accessed February 25, 2018, www .backpackerguide.nz/8-best-air-new-zealand-safety-videos/.

97   **redefinition of an airplane "seat":** "Economy Skycouch," Air New
     Zealand, last accessed April 24, 2018, www.airnewzealand.com
     /economy-skycouch.

98   **and numerous tweets:** Figure 43: Sue Teodoro (@SueTeodoro),
     "thanks for the #skycouch @AirNZFairy," Twitter, May 23, 2016, 7:44
     a.m., https://twitter.com/SueTeodoro/status/734711476573765632;
     Figure 44: Emily Jillette (@EmilyJillette), "We had to fly @FlyAirNZ
     home unexpectedly," Twitter, June 29, 2017, 12:56 p.m., https://twitter
     .com/EmilyJillette/status/880469963739418625.

99   **the website AirlineRatings:** Lorna Thornber, "Air New Zealand Wins
     Airline of the Year Award for Fifth Year Running," Travel, Stuff, last
     modified November 2, 2017, www.stuff.co.nz/travel/news/98471746
     /air-new-zealand-wins-airline-of-the-year-award-for-fifth-year-running.

100 **"instead of the software itself":** All quotes this section from Jay
     Hallberg, telephone interview with Jay Baer, November 20, 2017.

103 **Valentine's Day 2015:** Penguin Wrangler, "Spiceworks, How I Love
     Thee . . . " Spiceworks, last modified February 16, 2015, https://
     community.spiceworks.com/topic/795524-spiceworks-how-i-love-thee.

Chapter 10: Talkable Generosity

105 **products decreased in size:** "Shrinking Sweets? 'You're Not Imagining
     It,' ONS Tells Shoppers," Business, *Guardian* (U.S. edition), last
     modified July 24, 2017, www.theguardian.com/business/2017/jul/24
     /sweets-are-shrinking-youre-not-imagining-it-ons-tells-shoppers.

107 **"an incredible opportunity":** All quotes this section from Anja Stas,
     telephone interview with Jay Baer, December 1, 2017.

109 **"our own spot in Sacramento":** All quotes this section from Skip
     Wahl, telephone interview with Jay Baer, November 8, 2017.

109 **purveyor in 2017:** Studio 40 Live Staff, "Skip's Kitchen Is Top Rated,"
     Fox 40 KTXL, last modified March 2, 2017, http://fox40.com/2017/03
     /02/skips-kitchen-is-top-rated/.

110 **factor is food quality:** Nur A'mirah Hassan Basri, Roslina Ahmad,
     Faiz Izwan Anuar, and Khairul Azam Ismail, "Effect of Word of Mouth
     Communication on Consumer Purchase Decision: Malay Upscale
     Restaurant," *Procedia—Social and Behavioral Sciences* 222 (June 23,
     2016): 324–31, https://doi.org/10.1016/j.sbspro.2016.05.175.

111 **tell their friends:** Figure 46: Ashley T, "Friendly staff, cute lobby, and
     when you order," Yelp, October 17, 2017, www.yelp.com/biz/skips
     -kitchen-carmichael?hrid=HVzNUgvc5q4_DvQWtDRVSA; Figure 47:

kyrabob42, "Good food, awesome atmosphere and if you get lucky," Google, last accessed February 25, 2018, www.facebook.com/pg /SkipsKitchen/reviews/; Figure 48: Kim Poulsen-Smith, "So good. Always consistent," Facebook, last accessed February 25, 2018, https: //goo.gl/maps/V9yXPX464WB2.

Chapter 11: Talkable Speed

115 **of a good customer experience:** Parature, 2014 State of Multichannel Customer Service Survey, 2014, http://paratureprod.blob.core.windows .net/wp-uploads/2015/01/StateofCustomerServiceReport_2014.pdf.

115 **when calling a business:** Jeff Mason, "How Long Will They Wait," *Velaro* (blog), last modified October 8, 2012, www.velaro.com /long-will-wait/.

117 **the automotive industry:** All quotes this section from Brian Benstock, telephone interview with Jay Baer, November 1, 2017.

120 **founded in 1919:** "History," About KLM, KLM, last modified June 14, 2013, www.klm.com/corporate/en/about-klm/students/students-history .html.

120 **"Have you found it?":** All but the last quote in this section from Karlijn Vogel-Meijer, telephone interview with Jay Baer, October 10, 2017.

121 **has been so successful:** Figure 50: Kostis A. Tselenis (@kotselen), "@KLM great airline, excellent service," Twitter, April 12, 2016, 7:09 a.m.

122 **"current and future needs":** "Customers 2020: A Progress Report," Walker Information, last accessed February 26, 2018, www.walkerinfo .com/knowledge-center/featured-research-reports/customers2020-1.

Chapter 12: Talkable Attitude

124 **"would only allow":** Kaleb Ryan, in-person interview with Jay Baer, August 5, 2017.

125 **company that empowers:** "Uberflip," Companies, LinkedIn, last accessed February 26, 2018, www.linkedin.com/company/uberflip/.

125 **"center on making things easy":** All quotes this section from Randy Frisch, telephone interview with Jay Baer, October 15, 2017.

129 **share documents on-screen:** "Share Your Screen: Share, Speak and Connect with Participants," UberConference, last accessed April 5, 2018, www.uberconference.com/screensharing.

129 **"not all day/haha":** Dan Lewis, "The Self-Aware Conference Call
Line," *Now I Know* (blog), last modified May 11, 2017, http://nowiknow
.com/the-self-aware-conference-call-line/.

129 **"get a lot of tweets":** Rebecca Greenfield, "Finally, Hold Music that
Doesn't Suck," *Fast Company*, last modified April 28, 2014, www
.fastcompany.com/3029611/finally-hold-music-that-doesnt-suck.

130 **most-discussed UberConference features:** Figure 55: Olivier Travers
(@otravers), "Just got to an @uberconference 1 hour too early," Twitter,
November 22, 2017, 11:06 a.m., twitter.com/otravers/status
/933411381059170309; Figure 56: Christine Bader (@christinebader), "I
stumbled on @uberconference looking for a new free," Twitter,
December 18, 2017, 8:20 a.m., twitter.com/christinebader/status
/942791739147825152; Figure 57: Hamed Abbasi (@iamhamedabbasi),
"The hold music on @uberconference calls is the coolest," Twitter,
September 5, 2017, 11:11 a.m., twitter.com/iamhamedabbasi/status
/905131221344243712.

Section 4: Create Talk Triggers

138 **"criticism of you":** Godin, *Purple Cow*, 58.

Chapter 13: Gather Internal Insights

141 **"at the end of the day":** Wright, *Fizz*, 150.

142 **"part of creating":** Blake Morgan, *More Is More: How the Best
Companies Go Farther and Work Harder to Create Knock-
Your-Socks-Off Customer Experiences* (New York: Routledge,
2017), 69.

146 **"cannot expect them to tell us":** Youngme Moon, *Different: Escaping
the Competitive Herd* (New York: Crown Business, 2010), 220.

149 **"you know, take action":** McDerment, telephone interview.

Chapter 14: Get Close to Your Customers

155 **approximately 50 percent:** "New Study Finds that 19 Percent of Sales
Are Driven by Consumer Conversations Taking Place Offline and
Online," Engagement Labs, last modified November 27, 2017, www
.engagementlabs.com/press/new-study-finds-19-percent-sales-driven
-consumer-conversations-taking-place-offline-online/.

159 **contact point innovation:** Nicholas Webb, *What Customers Crave: How to Create Relevant and Memorable Experiences at Every Touchpoint* (New York: Amacom, 2016), 22.

160 **does this regularly:** Tom Karinshak, in-person interview with Jay Baer and Daniel Lemin, December 1, 2016.

161 **"in the shoes of your customer":** Anja Stas, telephone interview with Jay Baer, December 1, 2017.

Chapter 15: Create Candidate Talk Triggers

163 **had been all along:** Michael Stelzner, "Word of Mouth: Getting Others to Talk about Your Business," Social Media Examiner, last modified May 1, 2015, www.socialmediaexaminer.com/word-of-mouth-with-ted -wright/.

171 **"so simple it's scary":** Godin, *Purple Cow*, 96.

Chapter 16: Test and Measure Your Talk Triggers

185 **the "observer effect":** "How Does Observing Particles Influence Their Behavior?," Futurism, last modified July 28, 2014, www.futurism.com /how-does-observing-particles-influence-their-behavior.

Chapter 17: Expand and Turn On

198 **acquired via word of mouth:** Sean Ellis, in-person interview with Daniel Lemin, December 5, 2017.

198 **need to be able to convince:** Wright, *Fizz*, 70.

Chapter 18: Amplify Your Talk Trigger

202 **"like walking advertisements":** Jonah Berger, *Contagious: Why Things Catch On* (2013; repr., New York: Simon & Schuster, 2016), 187.

202 **sales than advertising:** Word of Mouth Marketing Association, *Return on Word of Mouth*, September 2015, https://womma.org/wp-content /uploads/2015/09/STUDY-WOMMA-Return-on-WOM-Executive -Summary.pdf.

203 **"we let people know":** Werne and Eckert, telephone interview with Jay Baer, November 2, 2017.

206 **"new bathroom amenities":** Tanya Gazdik, "Q&A: DoubleTree by Hilton Launches 'Warm Cookie' Campaign," Marketing Daily, MediaPost, last modified September 13, 2017, www.mediapost.com

/publications/article/307325/qa-doubletree-by-hilton-launches-warm
-cookie-c.html.

Chapter 19: Create Your Next Talk Trigger

211 **"hard to say much about it":** Tish Grier, "GasPedal CEO Andy
Sernovitz on How Word of Mouth Will Save Your Brand—Live from
Word of Mouth Supergenius," WordofMouth.org, last modified July 20,
2010, http://wordofmouth.org/blog/gaspedal-ceo-andy-sernovitz-on-how
-word-of-mouth-will-save-your-brand-live-from-word-of-mouth
-supergenius/.

217 **damaged its brand:** Trent Gillies, "Why LL Bean Yanked the Rug Out
from Under Customers by Ending Its Lifetime Return Policy," On the
Money, CNBC, last modified February 17, 2018, www.cnbc.com/2018
/02/17/why-ll-bean-ended-its-lifetime-return-policy.html.

217 **free soft drinks:** Quotes this section from Werne, telephone interview
with Jay Baer, November 2, 2017.

219 **"service or claim":** Matthew Dixon, Nick Toman, and Rick DeLisi,
*The Effortless Experience: Conquering the New Battleground for
Customer Loyalty* (New York: Portfolio/Penguin, 2013), 6.

INDEX

#1MakeALiving events, of FreshBooks, 58–59

ABL (always be listening) mindset, 183
adding talk triggers, 217–18
advertising, traditional versus talk triggers,
    23–24
airline boarding process, 73
Air New Zealand, 96–100
Amazon, 116–17
Amazon Web Services (AWS), 207–8
Americollect, 89–91, 160, 189, 195
amplifying talk trigger, 201–9
    because statement and, 204–5
    evolving operations to, 207
    guidelines for, 207–8
    marketing mix and, 205–6
    media and influencers and, 206
    referral programs and talk triggers,
        distinguished, 201–2
    simplicity of talk trigger, 203–4
Anatomy of Buzz Revisited, The (Rosen), 26
anecdotes, 148–49
attitude. *See* talkable attitude
Audience Audit, 6, 19, 36, 156
audience greetings, by Penn & Teller, 75–77,
    153, 205

Baer, Jay, 25, 95
Basri, Nur A'mirah Hassan, 110

because statement, 204–5
Benstock, Brian, 116–17, 118, 119, 120
Berger, Jonah, 13–14, 202
Berra, Yogi, 110
Bilas, Jay, 66
Blanc & Otus, 9
Boushard, Alan, 103–4
Bowie, David, 24
Branco, Luisa Torres, 78
brand positioning, 144
budgetary obstacles, overcoming, 173
Bunt, Brian, 28, 29, 31

Callahan, Eve, 46–47
call center logs, 148
Call Kurt for a Shirt campaign, of
    WindsorONE Lumber, 28–31
candidate talk triggers, creating, 163–75
    budgetary obstacles, overcoming, 173
    complexity/impact of ideas, mapping,
        167–72
    to complicated complaint, overcoming, 174
    fear as obstacle to, 172
    identifying potential talk triggers, 165–66
    initial inertia, overcoming, 172
    measuring difficulties, 173–74
    people might not like it complaint,
        overcoming, 175
    questions to answer in, 166–67

car service model, of Paragon Direct, 118–20, 214–15

The Cheesecake Factory, 3–8, 26, 43, 175, 180–81, 189

chocolate chip cookies, of DoubleTree, 17–22, 26, 43, 63, 168, 180–81, 194, 204, 206

Christesen, Deanna, 90

Christie Cookie Company, 18

Clube de Jornalistas, 77–80, 172

coalition building, for expanding talk trigger, 196–97

Comcast, 160

commoditization, 218–19

competition, and conformity, 41–42

competitive positioning, 145

Complexity Map, 167–72

  acting incrementally, 169

  complexity, determining, 169

  high impact, high complexity ideas, 170–71

  high impact, low complexity ideas, 170

  impact, gauging, 169

  low impact, low complexity ideas, 169–70

  medium impact, medium complexity ideas, 171–72

  prioritization of ideas, 167–69

conformity, 41–42

consistency, 72–73, 194

Contagious (Berger), 13–14, 202

conversation tools, 30–31

Copperfield, David, 75, 76, 153

Cornell, Alex, 129, 131

Create Distinction (McKain), 25

creating talk triggers, 135–219

  amplifying talk trigger, 201–9

  candidate talk triggers, creating, 163–75

  commitment to customers and, 137

  customers, getting close to, 151–61

  expanding and turning on talk trigger, 189–99

  internal insights, gathering, 139–50

  mind-set for, 137–138

  obstacles, managing, 138

  testing and measuring talk triggers, 177–88

customer anecdotes, 147

customer churn data, 147

customer dinners, of FreshBooks, 57–58

customer experience, living, 159–60

customer experience enhancements, 25–26

customer interviews, 158–59

customer retention surveys, 145

customers, getting close to, 151–61

  customer experience, living, 159–60

  customer personas, creating, 160–61

  customer surveys, 154–55

  product or service usage data, 157

  sales conversations, interviews and customer service calls, 158–59

  social media conversation data, 155–57

  wants versus needs of customers, 152–53

customer service calls, 158–59

customer service team, and talk trigger creation, 143

customer surveys, 154–55

Darden Restaurants, 5, 175

Davis, Ray, 45

DeLisi, Rick, 219

differentiation, 23–32

  conversation tools, creating, 30–31

  customer experience enhancements and, 25–26

  customer types and, 35–39

  lack of, impact of, 24–25

  Purple Cow effect and, 24

  WindsorONE Lumber Call Kurt for a Shirt campaign and, 28–31

  Ziggy Stardust persona and, 24

Different (Moon), 41–42

Dixon, Matthew, 219

donations to Sugar Mutts, of Lockbusters, 48–49

DoubleTree by Hilton, 17–22, 26, 43, 63, 168, 180–81, 194, 204, 206

Dutch Boy, 171

EC Chantal clothing line, Ryan's hidden messages in, 124

Eckert, Matt, 54, 55, 56

Edelman Public Relations, 10

Effortless Experience, The (Dixon, Toman and DeLisi), 219

Elevated Citizen, 124

Ellis, Sean, 197–98

empathy. See talkable empathy

employees

  SEE framework and, 193–94

  amplifying talk triggers, role in, 208–9

  expanding talk triggers, role in, 193–94

  internal insights, gathering, 142

Engagement Labs, 9, 14, 155

Enterprise Rent-A-Car, 212–13, 214, 215

enterprise-wide implementation of talk trigger, 194–95

evolving existing talk triggers, 215–17

executive champion, for expanding talk trigger, 197–98

expanding and turning on talk trigger, 189–99

  coalition building for, 196–97

  executive champion for, 197–98

  internal momentum, gaining, 199

SEE framework, 191–95
  scaling talk trigger, 190–91
experience advisors, 37–39
extra fries, at Five Guys Enterprises, 68–70,
  170, 194, 204

Face-to-Face Book, The (Keller), 14
Falls, Jason, 213
fear, as obstacle to creating talk triggers, 172
Fernandes, Ivan, 78
Five Guys Enterprises, 67–70, 170, 194, 204
Fizz (Wright), 15, 141, 163, 198
Flanders Meeting & Convention Center
  Antwerp, 106–9
Flynn, Craig, 29, 30
Foster, Stuart, 18–19, 206
free drink policy, of Holiday World and
  Splashin' Safari's, 54–57, 203–4, 217–18
free meal, at Skip's Kitchen, 111–13, 173,
  193–94
FreshBooks, 57–59, 148–49, 182
Frisch, Randy, 125, 131
fundamental fans, 39

G2Crowd, 9
Garden Sleep System, of Hilton Garden Inn,
  163–64
General Motors, 61
generosity. *See* talkable generosity
Godes, David, 5
Godin, Seth, 24, 70, 138, 171
Google, 116–17
Google Maps, 211–12
Gorab, Glenn, 91–93, 152
Graduate Hotel, 63–67, 70, 173, 189, 194–95
Gretz, Kenlyn, 89, 90–91

Hallberg, Jay, 100, 101, 102, 103
headbands, of Uberflip, 126–128
hidden messages in clothing, of Kaleb
  Ryan, 124
high impact, high complexity ideas, 170–71
high impact, low complexity ideas, 170
Hilton Garden Inn, 163–64, 213–14
Hogshead, Sally, 25, 27
hold times. *See* on hold
Holiday World and Splashin' Safari, 53–57,
  203–4, 217–18
Horsager, David, 10
Hug Your Haters (Baer), 25
hyper-relevance, of word-of mouth
  advertising, 9

inconsistent execution of talk triggers,
  dangers of, 194
independence, of word-of mouth advertising, 9

In-N-Out Burger, 157, 208
internal insights, gathering, 139–50
  anecdotes, 148–49
  brand positioning, 144
  call center logs, 148
  company-wide involvement in creating and
    maintaining talk triggers, 140
  competitive positioning, 145
  current word-of-mouth and social media
    trends, 144
  customer anecdotes and megafans, 147
  customer churn data, 147
  customer-facing employees, involving, 142
  customer retention surveys, 145
  customer service, involving, 143
  ground rules for, 149–50
  marketing, involving, 143
  market research, 145
  Net Promotor Score (NPS) analysis,
    145–46
  product requests, 147
  sales, involving, 143
  team tasked with creating talk triggers,
    selecting, 141–143
  win/loss data, 146
internal momentum for talk triggers,
  gaining, 199
interviews of customers, 158–59
IT community support, of Spiceworks, 101–4

Jantsch, John, 10–11, 43
Jiffy Lube, 117
Jillette, Penn, 74, 75
joker gets a free meal, at Skip's Kitchen,
  111–13, 173, 193–94
Joshie the Giraffe, 72

Karinshak, Tom, 160
Keller, Ed, 14
Keller Fay Group, 15
Keys to the Community, 49
KLM Royal Dutch Airlines, 120–22, 148
Koch, Louis, 53
Koch, Will, 53–54
Krispy Kreme, 207

Lemin, Daniel, 151–52
L.L. Bean, 216–17
local merchants, testing methodology
  for, 183
Lockbusters, 47–49
LogMeIn, 197–98
lost and found policy, of KLM Royal Dutch
  Airlines, 120–22
low impact, low complexity ideas, 169–70
Lyft, 214

Manipurated (Lemin), 11
McDerment, Mike, 57–58, 148
McKain, Scott, 25
McKinsey, 15
marketing team, and talk trigger creation, 143
market research, 145
Marriott International, 213–14
Mayzlin, Dina, 5
measuring effect of talk triggers, 177–81
   deciding whether to kill ideas, 186–88
   difficulties in, overcoming, 173–74
   lack of immediacy and, 177–79
   observer effect and, 184–85
   online versus offline conversation,
     measuring, 185–86
   small community of customers, testing
     in, 187
   steady growth and, 178–79
   testing versus, 179–81
medium impact, medium complexity ideas,
   171–72
meet and greet, by Penn & Teller, 75–77,
   153, 205
megafans, 147
Meineke, 117
menu, of The Cheesecake Factory menu, 3–5,
   8, 26, 43, 175, 180–81, 189
Moon, Youngme, 41–42, 146
More is More (Morgan), 142
Morgan, Blake, 142
Morton's The Steakhouse, 71–72
Murrell, Chad, 68, 69–70
Murrell, Janie, 67
Murrell, Jerry, 67

needs versus wants of customers, 152–53
Net Promotor Score (NPS) analysis, 145–46
next talk trigger, creating, 212–19
   adding talk triggers, 217–18
   commoditization and, 218–19
   evolving existing talk triggers, 215–17
   new ideas, generating, 215–16
   reasons why talk triggers begin to fail,
     213–15
   shelf life of talk triggers, 212
Nielsen, 10

observer effect, 184–85
offline versus online word of mouth, 14–15, 156
O'Haver, Cort, 45
on hold
   American consumers refusal to wait more
     than five minutes, 115
   UberConference's hold music, 128–31
online software companies, testing
   methodology for, 182

operational differentiators. *See*
   differentiation
overpromising, 62

Pabst Blue Ribbon, 163
Paragon Direct, 116–20, 214–15
pass-along effect, 6
Passion Conversation, The (Phillips), 30, 73
Penn & Teller, 74–77, 153, 205
Pep Boys, 117
Phillips, Robbin, 30, 73
Pontiac giveaway, of Oprah Winfrey, 61–62
pre-appointment patient telephone calls, of
   Dr. Glenn Gorab, 91–93, 152
product requests, 147
product usage data, 157
professional services company, testing
   methodology for, 183–84
Purple Cow effect, 24
Purple Cow (Godin), 70, 138, 171

quick reference guide, 221–32

reasonable requirement, 61–70
   Five Guys Enterprises and, 67–70, 170,
     194, 204
   Graduate Hotel and, 63–67, 70, 173, 189,
     194–95
   Oprah's Pontiac giveaway and, 61–62
   overpromising, effect of, 62
recipients of word-of mouth advertising,
   advantages for, 9
Referral Engine, The (Jantsch), 10
referral programs, 201–2
relevance requirement, 51–59
   company positioning and objectives, talk
     triggers must support, 52
   FreshBooks and, 57–59
   Holiday World and Splashin' Safari and,
     53–57, 203–4, 217–18
remarkable requirement, 41–50
   competition-created conformity and, 41–42
   definition of remarkable, 42
   Lockbusters and, 47–49
   risk of turning off potential customers
     and, 43
   skeptics and, 43–44
   Umpqua Bank and, 44–47, 173
repeatable requirement, 71–80
   Clube de Jornalistas and, 77–80, 172
   consistency, importance of, 72–73
   every customer, every time, talk triggers
     should be offered to, 72
   Penn & Teller and, 74–77, 153, 205
   surprise and delight efforts, lack of
     repeatability of, 71–72

Ridiculously Nice Collections, of
   Americollect, 89–91, 160, 189, 195
Ritz-Carlton, 71
Rolling Stone, 24
room key, of Graduate Hotels, 65–67, 70, 173,
   189, 194–95
Rosen, Emanuel, 26
Ryan, Kaleb, 124

safety videos, of Air New Zealand, 96–97
sales and/or operations teams, and talk trigger
   creation, 143
sales conversations, 158–59
same is lame. *See* differentiation
sardine gift, of Clube de Jornalistas, 78–80, 172
scaling talk trigger, 190–91
Schwartz, Yoav, 125
Scott Bradlee and the Postmodern Junkies, 131
SEE framework, 191–95
   employees, 193–94
   enterprise-wide implementation of talk
      trigger, 194–95
   inconsistent execution of talk triggers,
      dangers of, 194
   stakeholders, 192–93
Sernovitz, Andy, 16, 211
service calls, 158–59
service usage data, 157
Shankman, Peter, 71–72
shrinkflation, 105
silver telephone, of Umpqua Bank, 45–47, 173
simplicity of talk trigger, 203–4
Six Flags, 55
skeptics, 39, 43–44
Skip's Kitchen, 109–13, 173, 193–94
Skycouch, of Air New Zealand, 97–100
social media, 14–17
   conversation data, 155–57
   direct spending on advertising on, amount
      of, 15–16
   offline word of mouth versus online,
      14–15, 156
   trends in, researching, 144
   what's happening with customers, social
      data to help determine, 156–57
Sofer, Jay, 47, 48–49
Sorofman, Jake, 72
specificity, 6–7, 20–21
speed. *See* talkable speed
Spiceworks, 100–104
Sports Illustrated, 66
stakeholders, role in expanding talk triggers,
   192–93
Stas, Anja, 106, 107, 108, 161
Sugar Mutts Rescue, 48–49
surprise and delight, 71–72

talkable attitude, 123–31
   all levels of organization must
      embrace, 131
   UberConference and, 128–31
   Uberflip and, 125–128
talkable characteristics, creating, 30–31
talkable empathy, 87–92
   Americollect and, 89–91, 160, 189, 195
   Dr. Glenn Gorab and, 91–93, 152
   employee ability to work outside scripted
      boundaries and, 88
   inconsistency and, 88
talkable generosity, 105–13
   Flanders Meeting & Convention Center
      Antwerp and, 106–9
   Skip's Kitchen and, 109–13, 173, 193–94
talkable speed, 115–22
   as continuously moving target, 115–16
   KLM Royal Dutch Airlines and, 120–22
   Paragon Direct and, 116–20, 214–15
talkable usefulness, 95–104
   Air New Zealand and, 96–100
   resources useful to customers, creating,
      95–96
   Spiceworks and, 100–104
Talk Triggers
   candidate talk triggers, creating (*See*
      candidate talk triggers, creating)
   The Cheesecake Factory menu and, 3–5, 8,
      26, 43, 175, 180–81, 189
   competitive advantage granted by, 22
   conversation tools, creating, 30–31
   creating talk triggers (*See* creating talk
      triggers)
   customer types and, 35–39
   differentiation, importance of, 23–32
   DoubleTree's chocolate chip cookie and,
      17–22, 26, 43, 63, 168, 180–81, 194,
      204, 206
   exceeding customer expectations
      and, 84
   Five Guys Enterprises extra fries and,
      68–70, 170, 194, 204
   FreshBooks #1MakeALiving events and,
      58–59
   Graduate Hotels room key and, 65–67, 70,
      173, 189, 194–95
   Holiday World and Splashin' Safari's free
      drink policy and, 54–57, 203–4, 217–18
   Lockbusters' donations to Sugar Mutts and,
      48–49
   marketing, distinguished, 165
   next talk trigger, creating, 212–19
   objective of, 39–40
   Penn & Teller's audience greetings and,
      75–77, 153, 205

Talk Triggers *(cont.)*
  reasonable criteria for (*See* reasonable
    requirement)
  referral programs, distinguished, 201–2
  relevance criteria for (*See* relevance
    requirement)
  remarkable criteria for (*See* remarkable
    requirement)
  repeatable criteria (*See* repeatable
    requirement)
  sardine gift, of Clube de Jornalistas,
    78–80, 172
  traditional advertising versus, 23–24
  types of (*See* types of talk triggers)
  Umpqua Bank's silver telephone and,
    45–47, 173
  unique selling proposition (USP),
    distinguished, 7, 191
  WindsorONE Lumber Call Kurt for a Shirt
    campaign and, 28–31
team tasked with creating talk triggers,
  selecting, 141–143
Teller, Raymond, 74, 77
testing talk triggers, 179–84
  local merchants, testing methodology
    for, 183
  measuring versus, 179–81
  online software companies, testing
    methodology for, 182
  professional services company, testing
    methodology for, 183–84
  10 percent conversation threshold, 181
  25 percent conversation threshold, 180–81
Thomas, Geoffrey, 99
Toman, Nick, 219
Triangle of Awesomeness, 141–43
trust advantage, of word-of mouth
  advertising, 9, 10
10 percent conversation threshold, 181
25 percent conversation threshold, 180–81
Twitter, 156
types of talk triggers, 84–131
  exceeding customer expectations and, 84
  recognizing talk triggers, 85
  talkable attitude, 123–31
  talkable empathy, 87–92
  talkable generosity, 105–13
  talkable speed, 115–22
  talkable usefulness, 95–104
  Uberflip and, 125–128

Uber, 214
UberConference, 128–31
Uberflip, 125–128

Umpqua Bank, 44–47, 173
uniqueness seekers, 37
unique selling proposition (USP), 7, 191
unlimited drink policy, of Holiday World
  and Splashin' Safari, 53–57, 203–4,
  217–18
usage data, 157
usefulness. *See* talkable usefulness

Vogel-Meijer, Karlijn, 120, 121

Wahl, Skip, 109, 111, 112, 173, 193–94
Walker, 122
Walker, Craig, 129–30
wants versus needs of customers, 152–53
Webb, Nicholas, 159
Weprin, Ben, 64
Werne, Paula, 53–54, 55, 56, 57, 203–4,
  217, 218
Westin Hotels, 20, 213
What Customers Want (Webb), 159
what's happening with customers, social data
  to help determine, 156–57
Wheaton, Wil, 49
Williams, Kurt, 28–29
WindsorONE Lumber, 27–31
win/loss data, 146
word-of mouth advertising
  cost-effectiveness of, 8
  hyper-relevance of, 9
  impact of, study on, 9
  inability to buy, 13–14
  independence of, 9
  lack of plan for achieving, 10–11
  offline versus online, 14–15, 156
  pass-along effect of, 6
  recipients of, advantages for, 9
  sales increase resulting from, 5
  social media and, 14–16
  specificity and, 6–7
  talk triggers framework for achieving (*See*
    Talk Triggers)
  trust advantage of, 9, 10
Word of Mouth Marketing (Sernovitz), 16
Wright, Ted, 15, 27, 141, 163, 198

Y Combinator, 158
*Youtility: Why Smart Marketing Is about
  Help, Not Hype* (Baer), 95

Zappos, 214
Ziggy Stardust persona, 24
zoo admission, of Flanders Meeting &
  Convention Center Antwerp, 107–9